Praise for *T[...]*

"Get ready to improve your love IQ. In this remarkable book, Dave and Jan Stoop give all of us the practical steps for learning how to love SMART. Follow their proven guidance and your love life will never be the same."

> Drs. Les and Leslie Parrott, *New York Times* bestselling authors of *Saving Your Marriage Before It Starts*

"Great marriages are both art and science. Dave and Jan Stoop have integrated both in a highly effective system, using the latest neuroscience, to bring couples more intimacy and happiness. Great concepts and very workable skills. I highly recommend this book."

> John Townsend, PhD, *New York Times* bestselling author of *Boundaries*; founder of the Townsend Institute of Leadership and Counseling

"In the forest of books on marriage relationships, *The Emotionally Healthy Marriage* stands tall. Thanks to their years of professional practice, their knowledge of the Bible, the results of recent research on emotional intelligence, and their own vibrant marriage relationship, Dave and Jan have given us a unique and practical resource. The many Action Plans alone are worth the price of the book. No pie-in-the-sky platitudes or superficial solutions, but wise counsel that can make an immediate difference in your marriage."

Gary J. Oliver, ThM, PhD, executive director of the Center for Healthy Relationships; professor of psychology and practical theology at John Brown University; coauthor of *Mad About Us*

Living
STRONG,
Finishing
WELL

By David Stoop

You Are What You Think

Rethink How You Think

Change Your Thoughts, Change Your Life

Making Peace with Your Father

People of the Bible Uncensored

Forgiving Our Parents, Forgiving Ourselves

Forgiving What You'll Never Forget

Living Strong, Finishing Well

By David and Jan Stoop

Just Us

The Emotionally Healthy Marriage

Living
STRONG,
Finishing
WELL

HOW TO KEEP GROWING AND LEARNING
FOR THE REST OF YOUR LIFE

DR. DAVID STOOP

Revell

a division of Baker Publishing Group
Grand Rapids, Michigan

© 2021 by David Stoop

Published by Revell
a division of Baker Publishing Group
PO Box 6287, Grand Rapids, MI 49516-6287
www.revellbooks.com

Printed in the United States of America

Library of Congress Cataloging-in-Publication Data
Names: Stoop, David, author.
Title: Living strong, finishing well : how to keep growing and learning for the rest of your life / Dr. David Stoop.
Description: Grand Rapids, Michigan : Revell, a division of Baker Publishing Group, 2021.
Identifiers: LCCN 2021004375 | ISBN 9780800740184 (paperback) | ISBN 9780800741266 (casebound) | ISBN 9781493432028 (ebook)
Subjects: LCSH: Middle-aged persons—Religious life. | Older people—Religious life. Aging—Religious aspects—Christianity.
Classification: LCC BV4579.5 .S745 2021 | DDC 248.8/4—dc23
LC record available at https://lccn.loc.gov/2021004375

The author is represented by WordServe Literary Group, www.wordserveliterary.com.

21 22 23 24 25 26 27   7 6 5 4 3 2 1

In keeping with biblical principles of creation stewardship, Baker Publishing Group advocates the responsible use of our natural resources. As a member of the Green Press Initiative, our company uses recycled paper when possible. The text paper of this book is composed in part of post-consumer waste.

Dedicated to the men who
have walked with me
at critical times over the years:

Steve Arterburn
Bob Battles
David Engstrom
Ron Ritchie
Jim Smoke

CONTENTS

FOREWORD

I am sad to open this book with the news that Dr. David Stoop, my good friend and colleague of forty years, died on March 10, 2021, while trying to recover from a stroke he experienced in the fall of 2020. He was eighty-three years old, and he and his wife, Jan, were married for sixty-three years.

I'd like to tell you some things about Dave. He was a pioneer in Christian recovery, an early champion of Christian counseling, a hero to those who followed his advice and teaching, and a great man who helped millions through his practice as a Christian therapist, international lecturer and preacher, bestselling author and Bible editor, and a greatly admired radio counselor. His books and Bibles have sold millions of copies, and millions of people have listened to his wise advice on the

New Life Live! radio broadcast. He was a strong believer in Jesus and was one of the first to effectively integrate Christian faith and counseling when he became a clinical psychologist in 1982.

Dave was an ordained minister. He graduated from Fuller Theological Seminary and earned his PhD at the University of California. He was an adjunct professor at Fuller Seminary, where he taught courses in family therapy, and he founded The Center for Family Therapy in Newport Beach. Dave consistently lived out his strong Christian principles and faith with compassion and grace.

Dave authored or coauthored over forty books, including many bestsellers. *Self-Talk* was frequently seen in airports and bookstores all over the world. Perhaps his most life-changing work was *Forgiving the Unforgivable*. Some of his other books include *You Are What You Think*; *Change Your Thoughts, Change Your Life*; *Forgiving Our Parents, Forgiving Ourselves*; *Making Peace with Your Father*; and *People of the Bible Uncensored*. I was fortunate to be Dave's writing partner. Our first book together, *When Someone You Love Is Someone You Hate*, was the beginning of a collaboration that continued until 2020.

Dave's other writing partner was his wife, Jan—the other Dr. Stoop. Some of their books together include *The Emotionally Healthy Marriage*, *The Complete Parenting Book*, and *The Complete Marriage Book*. Jan is one of the brightest and most delightful people I've ever met. She has been by Dave's side to encourage him and at times to suggest that a project is meant for someone else. I have had a thousand dinners with them, and I think they are the most perfectly matched, mismatched couple I've ever known. Sharing about their differences at some of our New Life Ministries events has led people to understand that a healthy marriage is not about commonalities or compatibility; it is about acceptance, compromise, connection, and accommodation. Over the years, the two of them have modeled how to love each other in big and small ways.

Beyond the books he published, Dave was an astounding creator and editor of specialty Bibles. Dave and I coedited *The Spiritual Renewal Bible*, which was based on the seven keys of spiritual renewal and was awarded the 1999 ECPA Gold Medallion for Bible of the Year. We also worked together to produce *The Life Recovery Bible*, the most sought-after publication in Christian recovery.

I first met Dave in 1981. I had heard that he was the best Christian psychologist in Southern California, and I knew he was highly respected in the worlds of academia, theology, and church leadership. Dave and Jan came to a seminar I was leading, and that was the beginning of a relationship that not only lasted but grew deeper and richer over the decades. Dave became the friend I could count on to always look out for my best interests. He was the one I designated to share every weakness, compromise, fear, and shame. He was the safest man I have ever known.

The best part about my relationship with Dave was that there were no grudges, bitterness, or resentment between us—though admittedly I gave him opportunities to harbor a few of those over the years. In all our writing, Dave brilliantly expressed truth and always had the heart of the reader in mind. He wanted to slide in there with God's transforming truth, and his style enabled him to do that with some of the toughest characters.

We developed the Life Recovery Institute to help clinicians, therapists, counselors, and coaches understand the Twelve Steps so they would have credibility with anyone who was in a Twelve Step program. We did forty-eight hours of live recording, and it was worth it because the world will forever have Dave through these and other videos he has made.

When New Life Treatment Centers acquired the Minirth-Meier Clinics, I took over the radio show and began broadcasting out of California, changing its name to *New Life Live!* I asked Dave to join me, and he quickly became a favorite of our listeners. He wasn't just wise and respected; he was the big brother or father figure that some callers never had.

Over the past several years Dave served on the advisory board of the American Association of Christian Counselors, where he established The Life Recovery Institute. He was also on the board of directors for NewLife Ministries, where he conducted numerous workshops and intensives along with his radio-host duties. Dave and I also created the newly formed International Christian Coaching Institute.

As host of *New Life Live!*, each year I speak with hundreds of listeners who are "of a certain age." They've raised their kids, they have grandchildren, and they're winding down their career. They wonder if they've done enough, and sadly, many question whether their life has made an impact. But most are wondering about what they can do today.

In *Living Strong, Finishing Well*, Dr. David Stoop shares his wisdom and experience about this subject. Until his stroke, Dave continued to make an impact everywhere he went. He embodied the title of this book in a million different ways. How do I know? He did it for most of his life.

Dave never stopped learning and growing in the forty years I knew him. Even later in life, he knew he had some unfinished business concerning his own father, and he finally did the hard work to resolve those issues. When he did, it seemed to draw his own sons much closer to him. They traveled all over Europe together, laughing and loving life and strengthening their bond. I don't think that could have happened if there was a stubborn bone inside him.

I learned many profound lessons from Dave. First was the concept that "nobody changes." Dave let me argue with him for a while before explaining what he meant by that (and showing me why he was right). We are pretty much who we are going to be by age six or seven. Beyond that we are always who we are, and that won't change. What can change is the motivations of our heart; we can decide to love others well without selfishness. Behaviors and habits can change if a person has enough support to keep the changes in place, from the inside of the heart outward. Dave would say, "Too many people are waiting for some big change to overcome them, when what they need to be doing is setting in place peers, friends, counselors, and groups that keep them doing what they know they need to do." So, in a backhanded way he was saying that people change, but not in the ways we think.

The second profound lesson I learned was a bizarre statement Dave made to me one day: "When people have problems, it is the mother's fault." He then explained that the person with the problem most likely has yet to get over and beyond their mother. You see, if they had a great mother, they have to get over her or else everyone will be considered inferior to her and the way she treated her children. The opposite is also true. If a person does not get over a deficient mother, then there's a good chance they will subconsciously expect other women to compensate for her deficiencies. Either that, or their unresolved issues will result in constant conflict with everyone except their mother.

The third profound lesson Dave taught me brings us to this great book and Dave's advice about *Living Strong, Finishing Well.* Dave practiced what he preached. He did not retire into boredom. He stayed alert, active, and productive, and he enjoyed helping people see what they are unable or unwilling to see. No one was more qualified to write this book than Dave Stoop. If you don't yet have a strategy for your later years to bring meaning and fulfillment right up to the end of life, you will find it here.

I am so grateful for the opportunity to pay tribute to Dave. He was the best of the best, and I am a better person for having him as a friend for most of my life.

Stephen Arterburn

INTRODUCTION

I remember Ted. After his retirement, he was an example of someone who died before he was dead. Work had been his life, and he was very successful at what he did. Even though he never really liked the company he worked for, he loved what he did. He shared with me that he often wished he had ventured out and started his own business, but giving up the stable income had been too risky. So he acted like a company man until he reached sixty-five and faced mandatory retirement. Company policy stated that when you hit sixty-five, you got the gold watch, the send-off dinner, and a good retirement package. Ted was happy to end his tenure on good terms.

But he had no other interests, so after he finished his honey-do list, it didn't take long for him to end up bored. With nothing else to do, he started watching the endless cycle of TV news programs. It didn't take long for that to become boring as well. He had never taken the time to build deep friendships, and the few casual friends he had were still working, so they weren't available. He had no interest in golf or other activities, so he just sat around the house driving his wife crazy. More and more, he and his wife got into arguments. She complained that he was always in the way. So he got a TV for his home office and just hid in there. Soon the TV became his only friend.

Time took its toll on Ted rather quickly. He developed several physical ailments, and his kids noticed that he wasn't as mentally sharp as he used to be. They finally said something, but Ted figured dementia was just an inevitable part of aging.

If you were to meet Ted now, two years after his retirement, you would meet a man bored with life who seems to be just waiting to die. The truth is he already died on the inside. He is just waiting to physically die.

I also remember Marge. She had been the consummate stay-at-home mom. She had raised two boys and two girls, and even though they were all in their forties and involved with their own kids, she still called each of them every day. Her kids were all she talked about with her friends and with her husband. But when her husband died at age sixty-eight, she just stopped—she stopped calling the kids, stopped attending church, stopped attending Bible study, and stopped talking to her friends. She stopped everything and just sat silently in her chair—alone with her memories.

If one of her kids stopped by to visit, she would get up out of her chair and go to the kitchen to fix them something to eat. Then she would return to her chair. She reluctantly participated in conversations, and it was like pulling teeth to get a response from her. Friends stopped coming by because they said visiting her was too uncomfortable. She wanted to be alone, and she made that clear to anyone who tried to enter her world. One of her kids said, "It's like she's just waiting to die." In fact, she had already died on the inside.

Our Western culture tends to see old people as a nuisance. They require special care and patience. Their health is declining, and their eventual disabilities are only a prelude to death. They are frustrating to be around, they are forgetful, and they are often a burden to their families.

No one seems to honor old people like some Eastern cultures do. In such cultures, people honor the wisdom and experience the elderly have and seek ways to pass down their wisdom through the generations, often by shared living arrangements.

Our culture's tendency is to institutionalize the chronically ill, the elderly, and the dying as a way to provide caregiving. But by doing so, we lose touch with the wisdom and knowledge of the elderly, and we deprive the younger generations of understanding the process of aging. We also lose touch with our own mortality—something we don't like to think or talk about anyway.

As a culture, we crave being young. After all, it's the young ones who seem to have all the fun. "Growing old isn't for cowards," we say. We may quickly add, "But it beats the alternative," although not everyone agrees with that added sentence. We see aging as a gradual deterioration of the body and the mind. We fear that Alzheimer's and dementia are inevitable parts of aging. If we don't lose our mind, there's always cancer or some other disease to worry about. Like Ted and Marge, too many of us give in to what we call "the normal aging process." We see old age as a hopeless time because the brain slowly deteriorates and nothing can be done about it—it is just a part of growing old.

But recent research by neuroscientists has shown us new ways to understand the brain. Researchers say the brain has neuroplasticity, which means the brain can change; it can grow. Researchers tell us that there are ways to increase memory and mental acuity. Important parts of the brain can grow rather than shrink. The declines of aging are not inevitable. It seems they are more of a choice.

This means that our older years do not force us to face an inevitable decline, deterioration, and withdrawal from life as we've lived it. We don't need to die before we're dead! We can continue to grow and become more of what we are meant to be. We can have a growth approach to life and improve in areas we focus on.

Often, aging comes as a bit of a shock. Who would have thought we would become this old? Many of us are living longer and are healthier. But we haven't figured out what we want to do with the extra years. Can aging be more than a series of progressive illnesses or disabilities that lead to death? When people give up on their dreams, their goals, and their aspirations because of age, they risk dying before they are dead.

But those who are not intimidated by old age and who continue to live a full and meaningful life can live until they die. They are the ones who will finish life well. But finishing well doesn't just happen. It takes living strong in order to finish well. That's what this book is all about.

one

"IF YOU DIDN'T KNOW HOW OLD YOU ARE . . . ?"

Death is not the greatest loss in life. The greatest loss is what dies inside us while we live.

NORMAN COUSINS

The rest of the question asked in the title of this chapter is "how old would you be?" Some people in their seventies might answer the question by saying "ninety-five," while others in their seventies might just as easily answer "sixty." I'm told that veterinarians can examine a dog—maybe they look at their teeth—and can tell approximately how old the dog is. But I have yet to meet a dentist, or a medical doctor, or anyone else who can look at my teeth—or any other part of me—and tell me how old I am. The people who study old age all agree that no markers exist that define a person's age, except for their date of birth. So asking someone, "If you didn't know how old you are, how old would you be?" is a legitimate question. How would you answer that question?

We live in a time when technology and medicine have increased the span of life. We live longer and have the opportunity to grow and even reinvent our lives over longer periods of time. Conversely, technology allows us to squeeze more and more tasks into shorter periods of time. This is not spiritually helpful, because technology has made us very impatient with the slower process of growth. Genuine spirituality is a very slow process. Moses did not feel the stir of the call of God for justice until age forty. Moses had to wait another forty years to experience God in the burning bush. It was during his last forty years that Moses had the most to share with the people of God. Moses's most spiritually productive years were between ages 80 and 120. That is a long time to wait.

Today we are tempted to write people off as irrelevant by age forty. Instead, we should see our seniors as gifts to the church and to the world, treasures waiting to be discovered and mined to the depths. Those who are younger need them as mentors. Youth have strength, energy, and cutting-edge technology, but they lack the wider view of age. Mentors who have been there and done that can help those who are younger gain a better perspective on life. Without this healthy collaboration, the young are doomed to make costly mistakes they could have avoided. Mentors can also encourage the young to invest some of their energy into spiritual practices that may not pay off quickly but provide meaningful dividends in the future.

Mind and Body

While teaching at Harvard, social psychologist
Ellen Langer developed several fascinating studies that addressed the question of how our mind
affects our perception of our body and our age.
One was a simple experiment involving two nursing homes. Researchers gave each resident at
both nursing homes a houseplant. In one nursing home, the residents were given the responsibility of choosing where to place the plant and
when and how much to water the plant. They
were responsible for the plant. In the other nursing home, the residents were told the staff would
take care of the plant. And of course, since this
was a study, researchers gave a battery of tests
to everyone before the experiment began and
then again a year and a half after the experiment
concluded.

When researchers analyzed the data, they
found that people who had the responsibility of
taking care of the plant were more cheerful, more
alert, and more active. What surprised them,
though, was that less than half as many of those
in the group responsible for the plant had died
compared to those in the other group. The results raised a number of questions, especially the

question of how our mind affects our sense of age and the health of our body.

To address that question in more depth, Langer and her students developed what they called the "counterclockwise study." They wondered what would happen if they could turn back the clock and re-create the world as it had been twenty years earlier and then ask subjects to *live as though it were* 1959. (They did this study in 1979.)

Researchers found an old monastery in New Hampshire and worked hard to retrofit it so that it accurately represented the world of 1959. They chose sixteen men who were in their late seventies and early eighties. The men were randomly divided into two groups of eight—one group would participate in the experiment, and the other group would be the control group. Before the experiment, Langer's students did extensive testing with both groups, including measuring their height, weight, dexterity, vision, and memory. They also gave the men IQ tests and took photos of them to see if there would be visual changes in their appearance.

Once the experimental group arrived at the retreat, they were told to live, think, and act as if it were 1959. They discussed many of the political, world, and sports events of 1959. They watched

TV programs popular in 1959—on black-and-white TVs. They discussed the books and movies that were released that year and listened to the popular music of that year. After the first week, the men in the control group moved in and spent the week merely reminiscing about what life was like for them in 1959.

What happened? The researchers noticed a change in behavior and attitude in both groups before their week was up. By the second day, all of the men were doing things and working independently, unlike how they functioned when at home.

At the end of each week, the researchers re-tested everyone in both groups and found that the mind did have control over the body. Both groups showed improvements, but there was a significant difference in how those in the experimental group changed. Their hearing improved, their memory improved, and even their vision improved. They improved physically, becoming more flexible in their joints. Their fingers were longer and straighter, as their arthritis had diminished. They stood straighter and even walked better. They showed improvements in height, gait, and posture. They even looked younger. When asked to compare the before and after photos of each man, independent observers noted that the men looked noticeably younger in the photos taken at the end of the week compared to the photos taken at the beginning of the week.

Langer's conclusion at the end of the study was "to believe less and less that biology is destiny. It is not primarily our physical selves that limit us but rather our mindset about our physical limits."[1] Our attitude about how we age is everything! Live as if you are old and you will feel and act old. Live as if you are younger and you will feel and act younger.

Our attitude about how we age is everything!

Our assumptions typically are that as we age our vision gets worse, chronic diseases can't be reversed, and our mind deteriorates. We think everything is determined by the limits we place on our physical being.

For years, I have lived as if I were fifteen years younger. When I was fifty, I lived, felt, thought, and acted as if I were thirty-five. When I was seventy, I lived, felt, thought, and acted as if I were fifty-five. And then, when I read the counterclockwise study, I could easily relate to the results Langer found.

1. Ellen J. Langer, *Counterclockwise: Mindful Health and the Power of Possibility* (New York: Ballantine Books, 2009), 11.

If a group of elderly men could experience such changes in their lives simply by acting as if they were younger, what's to stop us from finishing well?

Is Eighty Really the New Sixty?

So does this mean sixty is the new forty or eighty is the new sixty, as some are claiming? Do a search on the internet related to aging, and you will find countless articles in which an age is declared to be a new, younger version of that age. Part of the discussion is based on the fact that we not only live longer but also act younger and are more active. As an example, take Betty White, who hosted a *Saturday Night Live* show in her mid-eighties. Or consider former president Jimmy Carter, who was building homes with Habitat for Humanity into his mid-nineties!

Questions like "Is eighty the new sixty?" weren't being asked in 1884 when German chancellor Otto von Bismarck decided to set the age of retirement at sixty-five. It was a benefit that wasn't used very often, for few people at that time lived that long. Life expectancy for men was around forty-five, and for women, it was only ten years more. So it wasn't that long ago that if you lived to sixty-five, you were considered old. Social Security was based on Bismarck's decision, and it was designed to ease us into old age and retirement. But sixty-five is not old anymore. In fact, there is a strong movement to consider people in their sixties as being middle-aged. What we think of as old is rapidly changing.

But all the talk of a certain age being a new, younger age ends up devaluing the older age. Generally speaking, people today in their eighties exercise more, are careful about their weight, don't smoke, and dress in more contemporary clothing styles, so they look younger, act younger, and even feel younger. But they are still in their eighties.

The reality is that eighty is well beyond middle age. It's much closer to ninety than to sixty. It's an age when we attend a lot of funerals, which only reminds us of our own mortality. It's also an age when we take all kinds of supplements in an attempt to stay healthy, and it's a time when we collect doctors. One of the good parts of being eighty is that we no longer worry about our résumé. Unfortunately, instead, we think more about our obituary. So eighty really isn't the new sixty; it's more like the new eighty.

Being the new eighty means we don't have to worry about trying to "become" something. Our kids are raised, and now we can spoil the grandkids (and maybe wish we could have had them first). At this age, we work because we love what we do. We are finally free to focus on

> **Eighty really isn't the new sixty; it's more like the new eighty.**

being comfortable with who we really are. And the new eighty means we are more determined than ever not to die before we are dead!

The Task of Midlife

The art of staying alive until we die begins with how we manage the task of midlife. Remember how certain questions sort of snuck up on you? Career, marriage, kids—all were doing well, and then, suddenly, questions popped into your mind without any warning. "Is what I am doing really important?" or "How long can I keep up this pace?" or "What's the meaning of it all, anyway?" The questions are natural, and they are part of what is called the midlife transition.

Erik Erikson, who developed the concept of the eight stages of human development, described the task of midlife as the experience of generativity, as opposed to becoming stagnant.[2] By this he meant that at midlife we search for significant ways to be productive, especially in terms of something that will last beyond us into the next generation.

It's also a time of evaluation when we look at where we thought we would be at this age and compare it with where we are. Have we met our goals? If we did, was it enough? If we didn't, now what? We ask ourselves questions like "What's the point?" and "Is this all there is?" We can end up evaluating everything from our job to our family members to where we live and go to church. Everyone goes through this process of evaluating their life to some degree. Some, unfortunately, turn it into a midlife crisis.

The person at this midlife point who becomes *disillusioned* begins to blame others for their failure to feel significant. They are disappointed with their career, with their spouse, with where they live, with the kind of car they drive. If only those things could be changed, all would be well.

The disillusioned person tries to fix the problem by making some major changes in their life. Do they need a new spouse, a new career, a different boss, a sportier car, a fancier house? What

2. Erik Erikson, *Childhood and Society* (New York: Norton, 1963), 266.

about new children from a new spouse? Anything that can be changed will seem like it needs to be changed. In their disillusionment, they actually believe that making these changes will help them find the sense of significance they need.

Of course, it all too often fails. Changing the other people in our life is like moving the deck chairs on the *Titanic*. The ship is still going to sink. Ultimately, such changes won't satisfy the task of midlife because none of the potential solutions deal with the issue of purpose and meaning. None of them deal with *me*. And because of that, we are in great danger of making major changes that appeal to either a pseudo-identity or a pseudo-intimacy. And finally, we end up in the same desperate place—stagnation without a sense of a meaningful purpose.

What we do at midlife lays the groundwork for successfully aging. Instead of being disillusioned with everything in our life, we need to stop looking at and blaming others, take the scales off our eyes, and accept the reality of where we are. The changes that typically need to be made in midlife are changes within us.

> **The changes that typically need to be made in midlife are changes within us.**

To successfully move through the midlife transition, we need to look within, asking ourselves what direction we can move in order to find genuine purpose and meaning so that our life will impact the generations to come. The successful transition of this adult stage of development involves being productive and creative.

Stepping into Old Age

Successfully navigating the midlife stage prepares us for the successful experience of what Erikson calls "old age"—where the task is to live with integrity. "Integrity is regarded by many people as the honesty and truthfulness or accuracy of one's actions. Integrity can stand in opposition to hypocrisy. . . . In this context, integrity is the inner sense of 'wholeness' deriving from qualities such as honesty and consistency of character."[3]

According to Erikson, ego integrity, as he calls it, involves coming to terms with who we really are. Our objective is to always be aware of what we can do to live an ongoing life of quality and purpose. We seek to accept our limitations but do not allow them to define our destiny. Our body

3. Wikipedia, s.v. "Integrity," last modified December 20, 2020, https://en.wikipedia.org/wiki/Integrity.

will age, our mind may decline, and our relevancy may diminish, but we can always refine the essentials of having a purpose in order to live a meaningful life. Remember, it's all about attitude!

But we live in a youth-oriented culture, and it can seduce us into behaviors that defy our struggle for integrity. Daniel Klein describes the "forever young" strategy as trying to deny the effects of aging by staying busy acting young.[4] There is nothing more undignified than an older person being caught up in the Peter Pan obsession with being young. There is also sadness in the father who wants to be like a brother to his sons, or a mother who wants to be an older sister to her daughter.

We live in a youth-oriented culture, and it can seduce us into behaviors that defy our struggle for integrity.

We need to step into this stage of our lives reaching for the wisdom that enables us to be wise mentors to the younger generations. That's an expression of integrity.

We must also come to terms with our regrets. Reviewing the past is a natural part of aging, and

4. Daniel Klein, *Travels with Epicurus* (London: Penguin Books, 2012), 49.

typically, a major focus of that review is our regrets. But when we get lost in the past and in our regrets, we not only lose our future but also run the risk of slipping into despair. We need to look at the things we regret and through hindsight ask ourselves what positives we can take away from those experiences. What did we learn? How do we find something meaningful and even restorative from our past mistakes?

I have identified seven principles that constitute living strong in order to finish well. We begin by looking more in-depth at how we are to live with *integrity*. Not only is this the task of old age, but it is also essential for finishing well. Principle two has to do with finding *meaning*. The third principle is *perseverance*—finishing the course. *Humility* is the fourth principle, and a *teachable heart* is the fifth principle. Sixth, we look at how *friendship* builds strength into our lives. And finally, we examine how *resilience* fits in. In each of the next chapters, we will explore one of these principles through examples, both from everyday life and through the lives of biblical personalities. In chapter 9, we will look at how to do a life review, and in the final chapter, we will look at the gifts of aging. Welcome to the journey of finishing well!

TO *Think* ABOUT, *Talk* ABOUT, AND *Pray* ABOUT

1. If you didn't know how old you are, how old would you be? Why?
2. What stood out to you in the nursing home study? What struck you most about Langer's counterclockwise study?

two

INTEGRITY

Son of man, these bones represent the people of Israel. They are saying, "We have become old, dry bones—all hope is gone."

EZEKIEL 37:11

Most definitions of *integrity* read like the first definition in my computer's dictionary: "the quality of being honest and having strong moral principles; moral uprightness." Being honest and having moral principles are important aspects of integrity. Wikipedia says integrity "is the practice of being honest and showing a consistent and uncompromising adherence to strong moral and ethical principles and values."[1] Again, there is an emphasis on being honest and having principles, but now consistency is added to the definition. Most definitions begin with honesty; some add consistency. Erik Erikson said that integrity is more than being honest, being consistent, and being morally upright.

When Erikson referred to the stage of old age, he called it the stage of ego integrity as opposed to despair. This is a simplification, but it could also be called the stage of self integrity. This stage of life begins when we tackle head-on the question

1. Wikipedia, s.v. "Integrity," last modified December 20, 2020, https://en.wikipedia.org/wiki/Integrity.

of our mortality. And part of that means we not only have to come to terms with the triumphs of our life but also must process the disappointments. Erikson said, "It is the acceptance of one's one and only life cycle as something that had to be, and that, by necessity, permitted of no substitutions."[2] Life has been lived, and there is no going back to change anything. We must come to terms with the disappointments and accept them in some way.

We can then define integrity as a sense of being unified, of being integrated, of being congruent with who we really are on the inside. This understanding leads us to see a person of integrity as a balanced person, as one who is undivided. This gets us closer to what we want to consider in this chapter. The word *integrity* is derived from the Latin word *integer*, which means "whole" or "complete." So when we are talking about the concept of integrity we mean the quality of consistency, wholeness, congruity, and honesty.

> **We not only have to come to terms with the triumphs of our life but also must process the disappointments.**

2. Erik Erikson, *Childhood and Society* (New York: Norton, 1963), 268.

Consistency means I am the same regardless of the conditions or the circumstances. I am able to make a conscious choice in all situations to be the person I really am. Honesty is intentional and thoughtful and refers to my adherence to my values and to being consistent with who I am.

The Lord used the word *integrity* to describe Job when he asked Satan, "Have you noticed my servant Job? He is the finest man in all the earth. He is blameless—a man of complete integrity. He fears God and stays away from evil" (Job 1:8). Neither Job's suffering nor his arguing with God destroyed Job's integrity. In his last protest, Job challenged God. He said, "Let God weigh me on the scales of justice, for he knows my integrity" (31:6). And God did know that Job had integrity. Job's protest matched what God had said to Satan in the beginning.

Throughout the book of Job, Job argues for his innocence and his integrity with his three so-called comforters and with God. God never rebukes Job for arguing for his innocence, only for having too small an understanding of who God is. At the end, God says to Eliphaz, one of Job's tormentors, "I am angry with you and your two friends, for you have not spoken accurately about me, as my servant Job has" (42:7). Job's integrity means that he was free to express a wide range of emotions with God.

Integrity—Becoming Who We Really Are

Throughout life, we typically define ourselves by our roles. When we were small, we were someone's child. As a teenager, we tried on different roles, some of which today are probably embarrassing. As adults, we often define ourselves by our job. Ask an adult man to describe himself and he will most likely first tell you where he works and what he does. In years past, women tended to define themselves by their roles as wife and mother. In the last fifty years, that has changed. Women may tell you about their kids or husband, but they may also start with their job, hobbies, or other interests.

What happens when we reach old age? We often don't know how to describe ourselves. An older person may tell you what they used to do or about their grandkids. If that is what they do, they are missing an opportunity to redefine themselves apart from the old descriptions. One of the often-unexperienced joys of this stage of life is that we can now define ourselves simply by who we are.

It's not always easy to do this redefining. We need to home in on the most important aspects of ourselves. How do I describe who I am without talking about what I do or used to do? My first attempt led me to say, "I am an old man in his eighties who loves his wife and his family."

This is a time when we should become more self-aware. We often begin this process by doing what is called a life review, which involves evaluating the different pieces of our past experiences (we will discuss a life review further in chapter 9). We can reframe the negative experiences by looking for insights and lessons learned. The results can add to our new, emerging sense of self. In the process, we may discover new goals and resurrect old dreams long forgotten.

One of the often-unexperienced joys of old age is that we can now define ourselves simply by who we are.

As we grow older, we need to find new meaning and purpose in order to become whole and wise. Instead of obsessing about the mistakes of the past, we need to grieve the what-ifs and the if-onlys, feel the emotional pain even if it's uncomfortable, forgive ourselves and others, and when possible make things right where needed in our relationships.

Perhaps the hardest thing to do in that list is to forgive ourselves. But if we can't or won't forgive ourselves, we stay captive to the past and miss the waiting journey of this stage of life. Only forgiveness can wipe the slate clean and heal the one who does the forgiving. It's a letting go of what and who we were in order to become who we really are.

Erikson said that "the lack or loss of this accrued ego integration is signified by the fear of death. . . . Despair expresses the feeling that the time is now short, too short for the attempt to start another life, and to try out alternate roads to integrity."[3] When we can finish life with integrity, death is no longer feared. Erikson goes on to tell about *Webster's* definition of trust—the first task in Erikson's stages of life. *Webster's* defines trust as "the assured reliance on another's integrity." Erikson then adds, "It seems possible to further paraphrase the relation of adult integrity and infantile trust by saying that healthy children will not fear life if their elders have integrity enough not to fear death."[4]

3. Erikson, *Childhood and Society*, 269.
4. Erikson, *Childhood and Society*, 269.

People with Integrity

Current examples of people with integrity can be hard to find. Looking for someone in politics with integrity is perhaps a futile search. It seems people have to be almost dead to avoid any last-minute disappointments regarding their character.

When I tried to think of someone with integrity, I thought of Albert Schweitzer, who had a distinguished career in medicine in Africa. He was seventy when the first atomic explosion was triggered, and the event moved him to become active on behalf of peace. In 1952, he received the Nobel Peace Prize. He traveled to Europe to lecture until he was eighty-four. At eighty-seven, he helped design and construct a road and a bridge near his hospital. He was true to himself and his values throughout his life, even into old age.

Other examples of people with integrity include Billy Graham, who over the years lived consistently with his values. So did Mother Teresa. For both, age was not a barrier to living with integrity and making major contributions to humanity.

In the Bible, I think of Gideon as an example of a person with integrity. God called him to rescue Israel from the Midianites. He hesitated and twice asked for a sign that God was really calling him.

Then he experienced God do the impossible in defeating the massive army of the Midianites with only his army of three hundred men. When God gave them the victory, the Israelites wanted Gideon to be their ruler. They said, "'Be our ruler! You and your son and your grandson will be our rulers, for you have rescued us from Midian.' But Gideon replied, 'I will not rule over you, nor will my son. The LORD will rule over you!'" (Judg. 8:22–23). Gideon knew himself. He knew his limitations. He knew who he was and who he wasn't, so he was able to resist the temptation and say no to the people.

The Old Testament prophets, beginning with Moses, exemplified integrity. Moses was eighty years old when God spoke to him out of the burning bush. He had retired at age forty when he fled from Egypt. For the next forty years, he worked as a shepherd for his father-in-law. Then God confronted Moses and gave him a new purpose, which was to liberate the Israelites from Egyptian slavery.

Note that God assigned all of the prophets impossible tasks. Moses was to confront Pharaoh, whose heart was hardened by God. Isaiah was told to "go, and say to this people,

> 'Listen carefully, but do not understand.
> Watch closely, but learn nothing.'

Harden the hearts of these people.
  Plug their ears and shut their eyes.
That way, they will not see with their eyes,
  nor hear with their ears,
nor understand with their hearts
  and turn to me for healing." (Isa. 6:9–10)

God's first words to Hosea were "go and marry
a prostitute" (Hosea 1:2). Not what you want to
be given as your first task. Jonah was told to "get
up and go to the great city of Nineveh. Announce
my judgment against it because I have seen how
wicked its people are" (Jon. 1:2). It's like they were
called to fail in their tasks. The only way they
could find purpose and meaning in their tasks
was by knowing that they (with the exception at
first of Jonah) had been obedient to what God
had called them to.

My favorite prophet is Jeremiah, who to me ex-
emplifies the meaning of integrity. He was called
to be a prophet in the year 629 BC and spent forty-
three years warning the people of Judah of their impending doom. Then he saw Jerusalem destroyed
by the Babylonians in 586 BC—and he watched as
King Nebuchadnezzar destroyed the temple.

Abraham Heschel describes Jeremiah as "a soul
in pain, stern with gloom. To his wistful eye the

city's walls seemed to reel. The days that were to come would be dreadful. He called, he urged his people to repent—and he failed. He screamed, wept, moaned—and was left with terror in his soul."[5] Yet through everything, he remained a person of integrity. He was true to his calling and was congruent with himself. He called the people of Judah to live with integrity in their relationship with God. He begged them, on behalf of God, "O Israel, my faithless people, come home to me again, for I am merciful. I will not be angry with you forever" (Jer. 3:12).

Jeremiah pleaded with the people to be reconciled with the loving God. At other times, he warned of coming destruction. But his audience never listened and never responded. He said to God, "When I discovered your words, I devoured them. They are my joy and my heart's delight, for I bear your name, O LORD God of Heaven's Armies" (Jer. 15:16). But then he asked, "Why then does my suffering continue? Why is my wound so incurable? Your help seems as uncertain as a seasonal brook, like a spring that has gone dry" (15:18).

At one point, he tried to stop conveying God's message to the people. He said, "But if I say I'll

5. Abraham Heschel, *The Prophets* (New York: Harper & Row, 1962), 133–34.

never mention the LORD or speak in his name, his word burns in my heart like a fire. It's like a fire in my bones! I am worn out trying to hold it in! I can't do it!" (Jer. 20:9).

When Jerusalem fell, the people were taken to Babylonia to live in exile. Jeremiah was left behind, and in the depths of his grief, he wrote, "Jerusalem, once so full of people, is now deserted. She who was once great among the nations now sits alone like a widow. Once the queen of all the earth, she is now a slave" (Lam. 1:1). And then the reality hit him, and Jeremiah described himself in the grip of a deep sadness and depression. He said that God had filled him with bitterness.

> He has made me chew on gravel.
>   He has rolled me in the dust.
> Peace has been stripped away,
>   and I have forgotten what prosperity is.
> I cry out, "My splendor is gone!
>   Everything I had hoped for from the
>   LORD is lost!"
>
> The thought of my suffering and
>   homelessness
>   is bitter beyond words.
> I will never forget this awful time,
>   as I grieve over my loss.

> Yet I still dare to hope
> when I remember this:
>
> The faithful love of the LORD never ends!
> His mercies never cease.
> Great is his faithfulness;
> his mercies begin afresh each morning.
> I say to myself, "The LORD is my
> inheritance;
> therefore, I will hope in him!" (3:16–24)

Jeremiah had integrity. In all his struggles in his role as a prophet, he never gave up. He was ridiculed, mocked, laughed at, and abused, yet through it all, he was true to himself and truthful with God. He knew himself well and was free to speak what he thought and to feel what he felt. There was no pretense in him. He was who he was! He could speak honestly with the Lord and with himself. And he could move from the depths of despair—"Everything I had hoped for from the LORD is lost"—to one of the greatest statements of faith: "I will hope in him!" He knew where to focus his hope.

A little over a hundred years later, after the Persian Empire had defeated the Babylonians, a strange event took place in the palace of King Xerxes, who ruled over a kingdom that stretched from India to Ethiopia. He gave a great banquet for everyone at the end of a celebration for their success. On day seven of the banquet, he decided to show off the beauty of Queen Vashti. So he invited her to come to the banquet wearing her royal crown. But she refused the request. As a result, she was banished forever from the presence of the king, and a new queen was to be chosen. The search for the new queen brought Esther to the palace, and she won the crown. She was chosen as the new queen. No one knew she was a Jew, and she kept this secret at the insistence of her cousin Mordecai, who was a palace official.

Jeremiah had integrity. He knew himself well and was free to speak what he thought and to feel what he felt. There was no pretense in him. He was who he was!

At the same time, a man named Haman was promoted to the second-most-powerful position in the kingdom—second only to the king. In his new position, he believed everyone in the kingdom should bow to him whenever he passed by.

But Mordecai, as a Jew, would not bow to Haman. This infuriated Haman to the point that he got the king to issue a decree that on a certain day all the Jews in the kingdom would be slaughtered. Mordecai told Esther about the plan and reminded her that she would die as well if she didn't act and talk to the king. He made the profound statement, "Who knows if perhaps you were made queen for just such a time as this?" (Esther 4:14). Esther's response shows she was a person of integrity. She told Mordecai to have all the Jews fast for three days and nights. Then "I will go in to see the king. If I must die, I must die" (4:16). She knew that entering the king's inner court without being invited could mean death, but she was willing to face the possibility of her own death to save her people.

Finally, Haman had had it with Mordecai and intended to kill him the next day. But God had other plans. Esther saved the lives of the Jews, the king ordered that Haman be executed, and Mordecai was made prime minister! To this day, Jews all over the world celebrate these events at the Feast of Purim. All because God raised up Esther as a person of integrity.

The psalmist asserts that "joyful are people of integrity, who follow the instructions of the LORD" (Ps. 119:1). Again, the psalmist says, "May integrity and honesty protect me, for I put my hope in you" (25:21). And David affirms that he "will lead a life of integrity in my own home" (101:2), which is probably the hardest place to live with integrity. Proverbs tells us that "people with integrity walk safely, but those who follow crooked paths will be exposed" (Prov. 10:9).

> **Let us affirm that we are going to live life with integrity so that when the end comes, we have fully lived before we die.**

As we age, let us affirm that we are going to live life with integrity so that when the end comes, we have fully lived before we die.

Finishing Well

I met Jim Smoke in our first year in college, and we hit it off right away. That first summer break we spent our weekends traveling all over the East Coast. When he transferred to a college across the Hudson River, we still did things together.

Jim was always involved in ministry in some way. He tried to get me involved in ministry as well. While in college, Jim had become the pastor of a circuit of three small Methodist churches in

the mountains in upstate New York. One weekend he asked me to preach my first sermon, and
I had to do it three times—once in each of the
three churches under his care. It seemed like I
talked forever, and I was sure I'd taken the full
thirty minutes I was expected to preach. But
when I checked my watch after the first service,
I found I had preached for only five minutes. I
remember feeling embarrassed by my five-minute
sermon, but when I said something to Jim, all he
did was encourage me. According to Jim, I had
at least gotten my first taste of ministry at those
churches.

The next summer Jan and I got married, and
Jim was on a preaching tour representing his
college. The next summer Jim got married. Our
wives became close friends, and our kids also became good friends while growing up.

When he finished college, Jim became a Youth
for Christ director in western Pennsylvania, and
it wasn't long before he got me into ministry as a
Youth for Christ director in western New York.
Eventually, we moved around the country for different ministry positions, and either he followed
me someplace or I followed him someplace, until
we both ended up in California. Looking back,
I think he gave more to me over the years than I

gave to him, but he'd have to be the judge of that, and since he's gone, he can't.

Over the years, he and I would often talk about how we wanted to finish well, both in our lives and in our ministries. These conversations were often started when the news reported that some Christian leader had fallen. We would try to figure out what had led to their fall and what we could learn from their experience.

When we were together, we tended to talk a lot. The last time we talked, just a few years ago, little did I know it would be our last conversation. Jim died a couple months later of cancer. All who knew him would agree that he finished well. He lived out his years with integrity.

When I've talked about finishing well on the radio program *New Life Live!* and at other speaking venues, people resonate with the concept. Recently, a listener challenged me. He said that you can't finish well without living strong, and I agreed—we must live strong in order to finish well. Finishing well starts early by making certain we live strong—and for starters, living strong means living a life of integrity.

TO *Think* ABOUT, *Talk* ABOUT, AND *Pray* ABOUT

1. Imagine you've met someone new and they say, "So nice to meet you. Tell me about yourself." How could you respond in a way that is different from your usual family, job, hobbies, or interests approach and instead home in on what's most important about you? If necessary, reread Erikson's definition of integrity.

2. What does finishing well mean to you?

3. What are some of the reasons Christian leaders and others don't finish well?

4. How can you develop ego integrity?

three

MEANING

The LORD has told you what is good,
and this is what he requires of you:
to do what is right, to love mercy,
and to walk humbly with your God.

MICAH 6:8

Viktor Frankl brought a whole new understanding to the importance of meaning in our lives. Much of his thinking was influenced by his experiences in a Nazi concentration camp during World War II. He was liberated at the war's end, and in 1946, he published his book *Man's Search for Meaning,* in which he shared his experience of being an inmate in a death camp. As a practicing physician and psychologist, he observed that many of the inmates experienced shock when they first arrived at the concentration camp, which was then followed by a sense of apathy in which they cared about only their own survival. But the apathy was like signing your own death warrant.

Based on his observations, Frankl made the claim that a positive attitude was essential for survival. He expanded on that claim and added that meaning can be found in every moment of living. Life never ceases to offer us meaning, even in suffering and in death. After personally enduring the suffering of the concentration camp, he was convinced that even in the most absurd, painful, and dehumanized situation, life has potential meaning.

I've noted in working with depression that a corollary of depression is a loss of meaning. Whether a loss of meaning is the cause or the consequence of depression, I'm not sure. But they do go together. That's why I try to get depressed patients to make some goals for themselves, even small goals.

Life never ceases to offer us meaning, even in suffering and in death.

I remember working with one woman, and the only goal we came up with was that she was to pick a day and try to enjoy being depressed. It was only for a day. Her assignment was to get somebody to carpool the kids to and from school, stay in her pajamas all day, eat junk food, watch TV, and even take a nap if she wanted. But all these things were to be purposely done as a way of enjoying being depressed.

She came in for counseling the next week and complained that she had failed. She couldn't enjoy her depression for an entire day. She said she got bored in the afternoon, got dressed, and got busy working around the house. She also said she noticed that she wasn't as depressed as she had been the week before. She had broken a depressive cycle, and from that day forward, her depression continued to lift.

This raises the question "What is a meaningful life?" I ask myself this question in relation to any person I'm working with in counseling. When did they lose a sense of meaning? I ask them, "What happened that made you feel so hopeless? Is there anything that could get you excited about getting up in the morning? What would give you a sense of fulfillment and satisfaction?" If we can begin to answer these questions together, their life might possibly change for the better. But it's no small order, for they first have to identify something that has meaning for them. And of course, they must want to change, which hopefully is why they are in counseling. Still, these are not easy questions to answer when someone is depressed or feeling hopeless.

How Did the Apostle Paul Face Hopelessness?

We typically don't think of the apostle Paul being depressed or feeling hopeless. Yet near the end of his life, he could have given in to feelings of hopelessness. Paul was in Rome, and his impending death was very likely. He had been sent to Rome as a prisoner, and while he waited for his trial, he was literally chained to his guards. No one would have criticized him for giving up. But he didn't give up—he didn't die before he was dead. He lived as he had always lived, and while in Rome, he wrote words of encouragement to the church at Philippi and to us as well. In fact, he wrote, "But I will rejoice even if I lose my life, pouring it out like a liquid offering to God" (Phil. 2:17).

What made him so fully alive as he faced his likely execution? We get answers from this last book he wrote while in prison. He begins with a sense of gratitude. "Every time I think of you, I give thanks to my God. Whenever I pray, I make my requests for all of you with joy, for you have been my partners in spreading the Good

> "Every time I think of you, I give thanks to my God. Whenever I pray, I make my requests for all of you with joy, for you have been my partners in spreading the Good News about Christ from the time you first heard it until now." —Paul

News about Christ from the time you first heard it until now" (Phil. 1:3–4).

He continues to share his attitude of gratitude as he writes, "I want you to know, my dear brothers and sisters, that everything that has happened to me here has helped to spread the Good News. For everyone here, including the whole palace guard, knows that I am in chains because of Christ. And because of my imprisonment, most of the believers here have gained confidence and boldly speak God's message without fear" (Phil. 1:12–14). He continues, "For I fully expect and hope that I will never be ashamed, but that I will continue to be bold for Christ, as I have been in the past. And I trust that my life will bring honor to Christ, whether I live or die" (1:20).

Paul never seems to have struggled with a sense of meaninglessness—partly because he saw everything that happened as happening according to God's plan. For him, everything had a purpose. In Romans, he writes, "We can rejoice, too, when we run into problems and trials, for we know that they help us develop endurance. And endurance develops strength of character, and character strengthens our confident hope of salvation. And this hope will not lead to disappointment. For we know how dearly God loves us, because he has given us the Holy Spirit to fill our hearts with his love" (5:3–5).

When Paul was sent to Rome as a prisoner and was held in chains awaiting his trial, which would probably lead to his execution, he must have seen his situation as an opportunity for growth that he accepted with joy. To the end, he anticipated growth in his character and in his hope for salvation in the future.

Finding Meaning in Everything

Paul's life definitely had meaning. He was called to a gigantic task—to establish the first churches. I was called to a lesser but just as meaningful task. I was called to pastor as an employee of a church, and I was called to be in ministry as a counselor. Both roles have given meaning to my life. In addition, I was called to be a husband, a parent, a grandparent, and now a great-grandparent—all of which have added meaning to my life as well.

But not everyone feels called to some public ministry or task. They still get up and face the day, doing a task that may not seem meaningful to them. They may feel like a little cog in a big machine. Or they may feel like anyone could do what they do. How do they find meaning in life?

Brother Lawrence offers us an answer to that question. He was a lay brother in a Carmelite monastery in Paris in the seventeenth century. His life was filled with seemingly meaningless tasks that had to be done so that the monastery could function. He kept the grounds clean, cleaned the kitchen, washed the dishes, and did other tasks that anybody could have done. But he developed a way to live his life so that the meaningless tasks became meaningful. In his classic book, *Practicing the Presence of God*, he describes his method for seeking God's presence in all his activities and consciously being governed by the love of the Savior.

For example, if he picked up a piece of straw that was on the ground, he did it on behalf of his love for God, seeking only God and his presence and nothing else. All the while, he was conversing with God. When washing the monastery dishes, he found satisfaction and purpose in the act because he was doing it for the Lord.

Purposeful Learning

Before we moved to California, I accepted a call to become an associate pastor at a church in Orlando, Florida. We arrived in our Volkswagen

Bug with our two sons at the time. I think we arrived on a Friday. Our furniture had not arrived yet, so we were temporarily put up in an apartment connected to the youth center. We had just settled into the apartment when there came a knock on the door. It was the senior pastor, Bob Battles, and he had forgotten to tell me something. He had already told us that he wanted to introduce our family to the congregation on Sunday morning, but he had forgotten to tell me that he wanted me to read the Scripture lesson during the service. His parting comment was, "Read it over at least three times out loud before Sunday morning."

It was the first of many suggestions I would receive from him over the next couple years working with him. Most of them were in writing. I saved them in a file. Some of the suggestions were learning opportunities for me in terms of what it meant to be a pastor. One I remember well was his suggestion that Jan sew up the pockets in my suit. That was his way of telling me it wasn't very professional to preach with my hands in my pockets.

We had a great three years of ministry at that church. I was always being challenged to expand my experiences and to learn new things about ministry. I don't remember ever feeling like I was being told what to do. Bob was my mentor.

A couple years later, we moved to a church in California, and Pastor Battles retired. On one of our visits back to Florida, we visited him and his wife in their retirement home. The real impact of his life on my life was laid out all over the dining room table. He had open books and open Bibles, with note cards stuck in many different places.

I asked him what he was studying, and he gave me a reply about a subject or topic. I asked him if he was speaking somewhere on the topic, and he said, "No, I don't speak that much anymore. This was just something that interested me, and I decided to dig out the answers to some of my questions." He was learning something new simply because he was curious and it had meaning to him.

His wife chimed in and said it was very common for him to have books spread out all over the dining room table. "He always has to be learning something new simply because of his curiosity." Learning new things gave his life meaning and kept him active and intellectually sharp. Retirement, for him, meant he had the time to look for the answers to many of the questions he'd had over the years.

A Personal Mission Statement

Over forty years ago, my wife, Jan, and I sat by a creek in the mountains and wrestled with an answer to the question "What do we want printed on our tombstone?" It was a time when companies were concerned with creating mission statements that described why they were in business. What was their purpose? So our tombstone question quickly became a question of purpose, and we moved to the idea of creating a mission statement that described our purpose as a couple.

What did we want to be known for? I had finished my doctorate (Jan would get hers later) and just started practicing as a psychologist. It seemed like a good idea to incorporate something about our focus as counselors. The mission statement we landed on was this: "to be facilitators of healing in people's relationships."

Over the years since, we have always evaluated writing opportunities, speaking requests, and counseling situations to see if they fit with our mission statement. What started as a potential message on a tombstone became a statement of what was, and still is, meaningful for both my wife and me.

What do you want to be known for? It's not too late to find meaning in this stage of your life. You may want to start with what you want your tombstone to say about who you were and are as a person and then turn it into a mission statement for your life. There is no wrong way to write a mission statement, and doing so will help you in your search for meaning.

What do you want to be known for?

Perhaps we can take a lesson from Paul and practice an attitude of gratitude and find meaning and purpose in everything that comes our way because it is an opportunity for growth. Perhaps we can take a lesson from Brother Lawrence and find meaning in even the mundane when we do it in the presence of God and out of love for him. Perhaps we can also take a lesson from my friend Bob Battles and find meaning in learning new things or finding answers to our questions.

As Victor Frankl observed, meaning can be found in every moment of living. Meaning can help us not just survive but live strong so we can finish well.

TO *Think* ABOUT, *Talk* ABOUT, AND *Pray* ABOUT

1. What do you do that brings meaning to your life?

2. If you knew you couldn't fail, what would you attempt?

3. What do you have to do regularly that feels meaningless? How can you bring meaning to that area of your life?

4. What could be a mission statement for your life? For what do you want to be remembered?

four

PERSEVERANCE

Stop at the crossroads and look around.
  Ask for the old, godly way, and walk in it.
Travel its path, and you will find rest for
  your souls.

JEREMIAH 6:16

As I write this, I'm eighty-three years old. That's old—at least that's what my body is telling me. I have the typical aches and pains someone eighty-three years old has. In addition, I have Parkinson's disease. I've had it for four years. The doctor told me that if I had to get Parkinson's, it was better that I got it at seventy-nine instead of at a younger age because I will not live long enough to get the really bad symptoms. But it has changed the way I work at the computer. I don't type anymore because two of my fingers don't work the way they're supposed to. I get a lot of extra *o*'s and *p*'s. So now I dictate.

The other thing that has changed is how fast I move. I walk slower now, and not just because I want to. It takes me longer to get into my car and even longer to get out of my car. It may even take me longer to get out of my chair, whether it is at the office or at home. I'm still counseling, although my schedule is about half what it used to be. I still do radio—two shows once a week—and I speak now and then, just not as often. Now to be honest, there are times when I would rather sit in my chair and nap or watch TV. There are times when I do just that. After all, I am sort of semi-retired. But that doesn't happen too often because I am committed to persevere and finish well.

Did you ever notice that the main part of the word *persevere* is *severe*? Perhaps that is why persevere means to continue in a course of action even in the face of difficulty or with little or no prospect of success. There certainly is difficulty in continuing a course of action when physically, with age, everything gradually begins to work against you.

There certainly is difficulty in continuing a course of action when physically, with age, everything gradually begins to work against you.

The Bible contains numerous examples of people who persevered. Noah persevered in building the ark in spite of the ridicule he received from his neighbors. David persevered for twenty years, eluding King Saul's attempts to have him killed. The prophets persevered, even though they were called to do difficult tasks and to persuade obstinate people. There was no glory in what the prophets were called to do, but they persevered and were faithful to the tasks God gave them. The one biblical character whose perseverance amazes me the most is Joseph.

Joseph Persevered in Spite of His Circumstances

Joseph's difficult situation started even before he was born. His father's other wives had already given Jacob ten sons, making him a very rich man. But his favorite wife was barren—no kids, no sons. Then God opened her womb, and she gave birth to a son named Joseph. He was the firstborn son of the favored wife, and he was born late in his father's life, all of which set Joseph up to be the favorite son. And he was. But this also meant he was disliked by his older brothers. Not just disliked but hated.

Then Joseph began telling his brothers his dreams. In those dreams, his brothers and even his parents bowed down to him. The dreams were prophetic—Joseph did not know how the story would end, so he probably just dismissed them.

One day Joseph's father told him to go and check on his brothers, who were watching the family's sheep. When he got to where they were supposed to be, his brothers weren't there. Now if I had been Joseph, I would have gone home at that point and told my father that my brothers weren't there. But not Joseph. He asked around to find out where they had gone. And then he went and found them.

This is how I imagine the conversation going between the brothers when they saw him coming.

"Here comes that dreamer!"

"If I have to listen to another dream, I'll kill him!"

"Why wait for another dream? We're out in no-man's-land. We could kill him and nobody would know the difference!"

"Yeah, let's kill him!"

But when Reuben heard of their plan, he convinced the other brothers to throw Joseph in a dry well instead. He secretly planned to rescue Joseph and bring him home. But while he was away, some slave traders came along, and the brothers sold Joseph into slavery. For a while, Joseph must have thought it was a joke gone bad, but then reality must have set in. He was taken to Egypt, put on the block, and sold to Potiphar, a high official in Pharaoh's court. Genesis 39:1 tells us that he was an officer of Pharaoh and captain of the guard. Some scholars think he may have served as the executioner. Not necessarily a great guy to own you.

Joseph could have played the victim. He was hated by his brothers. He was almost killed by his brothers. He was sold into slavery and sent to a country with a strange culture and a strange language. And that was only the beginning. He served his new master well and within a short time was promoted to be the head slave in the household. Then Potiphar's wife tried to seduce him, and when she failed, she cried rape. There was no trial. Joseph was sent to prison for a crime he hadn't committed. And then he was forgotten.

Joseph was seventeen when he was sold into slavery. Let's say it took him, at most, five years to become the head slave. That means he would have been twenty-two when he was sent to prison. He was thirty when he was finally freed, so he was in prison at least eight years. That's a long time. But God had a purpose, and he used that time to shape Joseph into the man he was to become. Proverbs 30:21–22 says, "There are three things that make the earth tremble—no, four it cannot endure: a slave who becomes a king . . ." Joseph was a slave who was destined to become the second most powerful man in the world. Surely, there were things God needed him to learn so that he would be ready to lead.

At one point, Pharaoh's chief baker and chief cupbearer were both put in the prison where Joseph was being held, and each man had a disturbing dream while there. Joseph saw that they were troubled and offered to interpret their dreams. The cupbearer told his dream first, and Joseph said it meant he would be released after three days and restored to his position. Joseph also asked the cupbearer to remember him once he had been set free and to ask Pharaoh to release him as well. Then the chief baker told his dream, and Joseph told him that three days later Pharaoh would order him to be executed. Joseph's interpretations both proved correct; however, two years passed before the cupbearer told Pharaoh about him. I guess God wasn't finished with Joseph yet.

Injustice piled on injustice, yet Joseph was faithful along the way, seemingly never giving in to despair. Now, he wouldn't be human if he didn't have doubts and questions at various points of his experience. Yet he always excelled, even taking over the running of the prison while he was there. And don't forget, he didn't know the end from the beginning. Everything was unfolding as time moved forward.

How did Joseph continually persevere, choosing to stay on the right path? We aren't told directly. But I think that Joseph practiced the principles of James 1:2–4 and Romans 5:3–5, even though they hadn't yet been written. Perhaps in putting up with his brothers' hurtful behaviors, Joseph learned that "when troubles of any kind come your way, consider it an opportunity for great joy. For you know that when your faith is tested, your endurance has a chance to grow. So let it grow, for when your endurance is fully developed, you will be perfect and complete, needing nothing" (James 1:2–4).

Perhaps God also taught him what the apostle Paul later said: "We can rejoice, too, when we run into problems and trials, for we know that they help us develop endurance. And endurance develops strength of character, and character strengthens our confident hope of salvation. And this hope will not lead to disappointment. For we know how dearly God loves us, because he has given us the Holy Spirit to fill our hearts with his love" (Rom. 5:3–5). This attitude became a part of the strength of his character.

Also, Joseph must have had an amazing relationship with God. Moment by moment, he made the choice to take "the old, godly way," as Jeremiah suggested (Jer. 6:16). He certainly lived as a man whose soul was at rest, in spite of the circumstances. Nothing could make him forsake that path. Oh, he certainly had times when he wrestled with doing what was right versus doing what was convenient. But the truth is that he stayed on course! He persevered!

Like Joseph, we too can be faithful and persevere without knowing how our stories will end.

I love the story of Joseph because it challenges my need to know the end of the story before I will trust the situation. Joseph was faithful without knowing how his story would end. That's perseverance. Like Joseph, we too can be faithful and persevere without knowing how our stories will end.

Ruth and Naomi

The story of Ruth and Naomi is quite a contrast to the story of Joseph. Bad things happen to the main characters in both accounts, but their reactions are quite different. Ruth and Naomi lived during the period of the judges, and their story began with a famine in the land of Judah that caused Naomi and her family to leave Bethlehem and move to the country of Moab.

Not long after they settled in Moab, Elimelech, Naomi's husband, died. They weren't in Judah, so there was no tradition for her to remarry. So she stayed a widow. Her two sons grew into manhood and both married Moabite women. At least Naomi had her two sons to provide for her family. But then ten years later, both sons died, and Naomi was left with only her two daughters-in-law.

Eventually, the famine in Judah was over, and Naomi was ready to begin the journey back home. She realized she didn't have much to offer her daughters-in-law, so she strongly suggested they return to the homes of their mothers. She told them, "Go back to your mothers' homes. And may the LORD reward you for your kindness to your husbands and to me. May the LORD bless you with the security of another marriage" (Ruth 1:8–9). But the two daughters-in-law insisted on going with her.

Naomi became more insistent, saying, "Why should you go on with me? Can I still give birth to other sons who could grow up to be your husbands? No, my daughters, return to your parents' homes, for I am too old to marry again. . . . Things are far more bitter for me than for you, because the LORD himself has raised his fist against me"

(Ruth 1:11–13). Orpah left and returned home, but Ruth committed to staying with Naomi.

When Ruth and Naomi arrived in Bethlehem, people remembered Naomi, and the entire town was excited about her return. They said, "Is it really Naomi?" (Ruth 1:19). We see the bitterness that flowed out of Naomi when she replied, "Don't call me Naomi. . . . Instead, call me Mara" (1:20). Naomi means "pleasant," but Mara means "bitter." Naomi was saying to her people, "Don't call me Pleasant. My name is now Bitter!"

I like the story of Naomi. It's a more common experience that when bad things happen over and over, people become bitter and resentful. They don't excel as Joseph did. What's the hope for them? That's a question Naomi's experience answers. Her bitterness grew over time because bad things happened to her as she aged. She was in danger of becoming a bitter old woman; maybe she had already become one. But then God made her daughter-in-law stick to her like glue, and she had to get busy and give her a new life in Bethlehem.

The story of Naomi wasn't over; there was more to come. Through a series of events, and through interesting courting rituals that were apparently unique to that period of time, Naomi rose above the events of her life and found a new purpose. Naomi found Ruth a new husband named Boaz.

Boaz and Ruth married and had a son named Obed. And that meant Naomi had a grandson! He was in fact the grandfather of King David. Naomi stayed the course in spite of her bitterness and found something that gave her life meaning again. The psalmist reminds us that "even in old age they [the godly] will still produce fruit; they will remain vital and green" (Ps. 92:14). People can be fruitful and persevere even in old age.

> "Even in old age they [the godly] will still produce fruit; they will remain vital and green." (Ps. 92:14)

David Meets David

When I was in high school, I wasn't interested in being obedient. I was interested in doing what I wanted to do. At least that was true during the week—on Sundays I would clean up my act, and often I would even play the organ in Sunday morning church. The rest of the week was up for grabs.

I started my high school days in the upper third of my class, and I finished my high school career in the bottom third of my class. And I always said that I had a lot of fun on the way down. I didn't realize until later that there were consequences for my behavior. I couldn't get into any of the colleges of my choice because my grades were so bad. I never let my children read my high school year-book because my classmates described too many embarrassing things that I did.

But there was one thing that kept me from straying too far off course, and that was an old man (especially to a high school senior) in the church named David Engstrom. He would have been my grandfather's age. For some reason, he took an interest in me. He said it was because both our names were David. I have never forgot-ten him or the impact he had on my growth and development as a man.

I don't think we ever had profound, in-depth conversations. We never discussed complicated theological concepts. In fact, I don't remember anything memorable from our conversations. He simply wanted to get to know me and show me that it was okay to just be me. He seemed to know there was a battle going on inside me between following God's path for my life and going it on my own. He made me feel like I was a person worth knowing. This was pretty important for a mixed-up kid.

The summer after my graduation from high school, I was hanging out at our church's summer camp. It was an amazing summer; even A. W. Tozer preached. But I don't remember listening to his sermon. I was too busy arguing with myself. Do I go God's way? Or do I turn my back on God and go my own way? I chose God's way, and to this day, I believe that David Engstrom was the major factor in helping me make the right choice and persevere.

Persevering enables us to live strong so as to finish well.

TO *Think* ABOUT, *Talk* ABOUT, AND *Pray* ABOUT

1. How have you typically defined perseverance? Have you included the severe aspects of perseverance in your definition?

2. In what areas of your life have you struggled with, or are currently struggling with, persevering?

3. How can you persevere in this stage of your life in order to finish well?

five

HUMILITY

All of you, clothe yourselves with
humility toward one another, because,
"God opposes the proud,
but shows favor to the humble."

1 PETER 5:5 NIV

Humility is a fascinating personality trait. The more you think you've achieved some humility, the more it slips away and pride takes its place. I remember sitting around in college jokingly brainstorming with my friends about the books we were going to write. Someone suggested the title *Humility and How I Achieved It*. We laughed. Then someone suggested a pseudonym for the author: I. M. Humble. We laughed some more. It's an old joke, but it illustrates the elusive character of humility. When we think we have achieved it, we have lost it. We can possess the trait only when we don't think we possess it. It's hard to be proud about being humble.

In his first letter to the churches in what is now Turkey, Peter wrote, "Clothe yourselves with humility" (1 Pet. 5:5 NIV). As he looked at what he had written, I wonder if he had to lay down his pen. Perhaps he was flooded with memories of the last supper he had eaten with Jesus before the crucifixion. What had started out as a discussion among the disciples about who would betray Jesus had quickly gone back to an ongoing argument about who was going to be the number one disciple in Jesus's kingdom. Luke puts it this way: "Then they began to argue among themselves about who would be the greatest among them" (Luke 22:24). Let's set the scene.

The roads in Palestine were dirt roads. That meant that in dry seasons the dirt was dust, and in wet seasons the dirt was mud. And since you would not want to track dust or mud into anyone's home, a slave was posted by the door to wash the feet of anyone coming to the house—if the owner could afford one. If the host didn't have a slave, those entering the house would wash one another's feet. It doesn't take much to imagine that on this night when the disciples knew Jesus was about to act and were arguing over which of them would be number one in his kingdom, no one in their group was about to wash anybody else's feet.

As they sat down around the table, they all tried to hide their dirty feet. And whatever else they did, they were careful not to look at the pitcher of water or the stack of towels on the table by the door. The apostle John picks up the story: "He [Jesus] got up from the table, took off his robe, wrapped a towel around his waist, and poured water into a basin. Then he began to wash the disciples' feet, drying them with the towel he

had wrapped around him" (John 13:4–5). The way
John describes Jesus, to all outward appearances,
he looked and acted like a slave.

One can easily imagine what was going
through Peter's mind. Self-deprecating thoughts
like condemning himself for letting things get
so out of control. Or perhaps he was thinking
back to that time not too long ago when he had
confessed to Jesus, "You are the Messiah, the
Son of the living God" (Matt. 16:16). Impetuous
Peter was trapped. Why hadn't he stopped Jesus
right away? When Jesus came to him, he had run
out of options. John describes the scene: "When
Jesus came to Simon Peter, Peter said to him,
'Lord, are you going to wash my feet?'" If you
don't know what else to do or say, ask a question.
"Jesus replied, 'You don't understand now what I
am doing, but someday you will.'" As a matter of
pride, Peter said to Jesus, "No, . . . you will never
ever wash my feet!" (John 13:6–8). We could add
to his comment, "I know who you are. You are the
Lord of the universe, and you think you can wash
my feet? Never! I should be washing your feet!"

Peter was cornered. Here was the Lord of the
universe looking and acting like a slave, waiting
for Peter to let him wash his feet. Then Jesus told
him, "Unless I wash you, you won't belong to me,"

to which Peter responded in his typical Peter way, "Then wash my hands and head as well, Lord, not just my feet!" (John 13:8–9). Jesus reminded him that he had already bathed and needed only his feet washed.

Jesus turned an awkward and embarrassing situation into a powerful lesson on humility. John records how Jesus put his robe back on, sat back down, and asked this question: "Do you understand what I was doing? You call me 'Teacher' and 'Lord,' and you are right, because that's what I am. And since I, your Lord and Teacher, have washed your feet, you ought to wash each other's feet. I have given you an example to follow. Do as I have done to you. I tell you the truth, slaves are not greater than their master. Nor is the messenger more important than the one who sends the message. Now that you know these things, God will bless you for doing them" (John 13:12–17). Jesus was explaining how his followers are to live— clothed in humility. Undoubtedly, Peter got the point.

Humility Defined

Each of us has struggled in our own way with seeking to understand how humility fits into our life. My struggle with humility came to a head in the early days of my ministry when I was the local Youth for Christ director in western New York. When a pastor was gone from his pulpit, I was frequently asked to preach for him. And when I finished preaching, I tried to apply what I understood to be the meaning of humility. As people would shake my hand after the service was over, many of them would compliment me on my sermon, whether deserved or not, and I would say to them, "Give God the glory."

One Sunday one of the older saints took me aside and told me that when I said to give God the glory, I was negating what people wanted to say to me. They were not concerned about humility; they were expressing appreciation. Then he suggested I say something simple in response like "Thank you."

I thanked him and said I would work on it. At first, I felt awkward saying thank you, feeling as if I was robbing God of the glory. Then, gradually, I began to notice I felt freer to simply interact with the person expressing their feelings. But I was still left with the question of where humility fit in. So I went back to John 13.

What was Peter thinking as his turn to have his feet washed by Jesus drew closer? I would have been trying to figure out how I could come out looking good. I would have been posturing. Peter responded to Jesus with a question: "Lord, are you going to wash my feet?" (John 13:6). Well, it was obvious that that was what Jesus was going to do. Then Peter protested and told Jesus, "No, . . . you will never ever wash my feet!" (13:8). He was posturing for the other disciples. He was trying to justify himself.

One definition of humility is "a modest or low view of one's own importance." That's a pretty negative understanding of humility. I don't think that's what Jesus had in mind when he washed the disciples' feet. Nor is it what Peter understood based on his experience that evening with Jesus and his fellow disciples. In fact, based on John 13 and 1 Peter 5:5, humility has nothing to do with having a modest or low view of oneself. Humility is the quality of servant-leaders who have no need to justify themselves. Simply put, true humility means I have no need to justify myself. I have no need

> True humility means I have no need to justify myself. I have no need to make myself look good in the eyes of other people.

to make myself look good in the eyes of other people.

Someone Who Failed at Being Humble

To consider someone whose life revealed an absence of humility, let's look at Saul, whose story is found in the book of 1 Samuel. We first meet Saul after his father had told him to take a servant and go find his missing donkeys. Tradition says that Kish, Saul's father, was a general in Israel's army, so if he gave Saul a task to do, Saul had better do it. Saul and the servant searched the entire day and could not find the donkeys. Saul was ready to give up and go home and face his father. But the servant wasn't ready—there was one more thing they could try.

The servant remembered that in the town in which they found themselves there lived what he called a "man of God." He said that maybe this man could help them find the donkeys. Little did they know that they were really part of a larger plan that was designed to bring Saul to Samuel. The man of God turned out to be the prophet Samuel, and God had arranged for Samuel to meet Saul that day.

The leaders of Israel had pressured Samuel to convince God that they should have a king. They didn't want to be ruled by Samuel's sons. God had agreed that they could have a king, and Samuel was about to meet him. Samuel sent Saul and the servant ahead of him up to the place of worship, and when he joined them, he sat Saul at the place of honor and told the cook to serve Saul the finest cut of meat—both unusual. Samuel didn't tell Saul why he was doing any of this. Saul spent the night, and in the morning, Samuel sent the servant on ahead and then anointed Saul to be the ruler over Israel. To confirm what he had done, Samuel told Saul all kinds of things that were going to happen to him on his way home. And everything happened just as Samuel said it would.

But no one had asked Saul what he thought about being king. We get a sense of how he would have responded in how he introduced himself to Samuel. "But I'm only from the tribe of Benjamin, the smallest tribe in Israel, and my family is the least important of all the families of that tribe!" (1 Sam. 9:21). He didn't think much of himself. He approached life from a position of fear. And this was clearly seen the next time Samuel met Saul.

Samuel called for all the people of Israel to gather at Mizpah so that God could give them a king. "Present yourselves before the LORD by tribes and clans" (1 Sam. 10:19). The tribe of Benjamin was chosen by lot, and eventually Saul was chosen from among them. We can imagine the people cheering and clapping. And then the clapping ended and there was only silence. And there was no Saul. They couldn't find him!

So they asked the Lord where he was and were told that he was hiding among the baggage. They brought him out, and he was introduced to Israel. And then they went home, and so did Saul. There was no palace, no throne, just the title of king, and Saul was left with all the chores he had to do back home.

Sometime later, King Nahash of Ammon, Israel's enemy, came against the people of Jabesh-gilead. The terms of peace included gouging out the right eye of everyone in the town. The elders asked for a week to send out messengers to see if anyone would rescue them. When Saul came in from plowing the fields, he asked why everyone was crying. When he was told what had happened, "the Spirit of God came powerfully upon Saul, and he became very angry" (1 Sam. 11:6). He was no longer afraid. Healthy anger offset fear, so he mobilized the army of Israel and defeated the Ammonites. Israel had a leader. He was accepted as king by the people of Israel.

When we come to chapter 15, we see what developed in Saul's character. Samuel went to Saul and told him that the Lord had decided to destroy the nation of Amalek. And that meant the *entire* nation of Amalek! Saul carried out most of Samuel's instructions and was heading home when Samuel confronted him about his disobedience. Saul was very creative in his response to Samuel's charges, giving him a "spiritual" excuse. He told Samuel, "Then my troops brought in the best of the sheep, goats, cattle, and plunder to *sacrifice to the* LORD *your God* in Gilgal" (1 Sam. 15:21, emphasis added). When Samuel didn't accept that excuse, Saul finally admitted, "Yes, I have sinned. I have disobeyed your instructions and the LORD's command, for *I was afraid of the people* and did what they demanded. But now, please forgive my sin and come back with me so that I may worship the LORD" (vv. 24–25, emphasis added). The old fear was back.

Obedience didn't matter as much to Saul as looking good in the eyes of other people.

When Samuel refused, Saul pleaded with him. "I know I have sinned. But please, at least honor me before the elders of my people and before Israel by coming back with

me so that I may worship the LORD your God"
(1 Sam. 15:30). In other words, "I need to please
the people." Obedience didn't matter as much to
Saul as looking good in the eyes of other people.

The Importance of Humility

In Deuteronomy 8:2–3, Moses reminds the people
to "remember how the LORD your God led you
through the wilderness for these forty years, hum-
bling you and testing you to prove your character,
and to find out whether or not you would obey
his commands. Yes, he humbled you by letting
you go hungry then feeding you with manna, a
food previously unknown to you and your ancestors. He did it to teach you that people do not live
by bread alone; rather, we live by every word that
comes from the mouth of the LORD."

Earlier, Moses was described as "very humble—
more humble than any other person on earth"
(Num. 12:3). David tells us that the Lord "leads
the humble in doing right, teaching them his way"
(Ps. 25:9). He reminds us that "though the LORD
is great, he cares for the humble, but he keeps his
distance from the proud" (138:6). Again, David
says that "the LORD supports the humble, but he
brings the wicked down into the dust" (147:6).

Solomon points out that "the LORD mocks the mockers but is gracious to the humble" (Prov. 3:34). He adds that "pride leads to disgrace, but with humility comes wisdom" (11:2), "haughtiness goes before destruction; humility precedes honor" (18:12), and "true humility and fear of the LORD lead to riches, honor, and long life" (22:4).

Paul summarized the entire question of humility when he wrote, "You must have the same attitude that Christ Jesus had. Though he was God, he did not think of equality with God as something to cling to. Instead, he gave up his divine privileges; he took the humble position of a slave and was born as a human being. When he appeared in human form, he humbled himself in obedience to God and died a criminal's death on a cross" (Phil. 2:5–8).

If the Son of God showed this much humility, taking on our sinful flesh, like a servant washing his disciples' feet, and dying a humiliating death on a cross, how much more should we follow his example and make humility a part of our lives? Humility is a characteristic that will help us live strong so we can finish well.

TO *Think* ABOUT, *Talk* ABOUT, AND *Pray* ABOUT

1. What do you think of when you hear the word *humility*?
2. What are some of the definitions of humility that are common in our culture?
3. How does the definition "not needing to justify myself" describe humility?
4. How can you cultivate humility in your life?

six

A TEACHABLE HEART

Physical training is good, but training for godliness is much better, promising benefits in this life and in the life to come.

1 TIMOTHY 4:8

For decades, we believed the old adage "You can't teach an old dog new tricks." Some people didn't believe it, so they tried to teach an old dog new tricks, and sometimes they were successful. The training just took longer. Today, with the understanding we have of how the brain works—even a dog's brain—old dogs and even humans can and do learn new tricks. And they can do so quickly.

Several years ago, I was determined to better understand how the human brain works. In my training, there had been no coursework on the brain. The feeling was that it wasn't necessary. But I became more and more curious about the brain, especially as new research was continuing to be done. I bought a book on the brain, but I had no framework to put the information in, so I gave up.

Then I saw an advertisement for a week-long conference on the brain held at a hotel on Hilton Head Island. I attended that conference and finally began to understand all kinds of things about how the brain works. One of the things that stood out, because it was repeated several times during the conference, was how to keep our brains young.

Three Things to Keep Our Brains Young

The consensus was that three things keep our brains young. First is aerobic exercise. Now, you may react as I reacted: "Not more exercise!" But then the researchers went on to explain that the exercise doesn't have to be strenuous; it just has to be aerobic, which means it oxygenates the blood. If you walk briskly for thirty minutes, four times per week, that is sufficient.

Second, the experts at the conference said we need some form of focused attention or meditation. Many researchers were drawn to forms of meditation that involved emptying the mind. Now, I'm not comfortable with emptying my mind. I think of the story Jesus told about the man who cleaned out his house and got rid of a demon. But he left the house empty. The demon came back and brought seven more demons with him. So the man's troubles were compounded.

The meditation spoken about in the Bible, in particular in the Psalms, is what is called *discursive meditation*. This type of meditation focuses on something meaningful—preferably the Scriptures. We are told to hide God's Word in our hearts (Ps. 119:11) and to ponder it throughout the day. God knows that our brains thrive on focused attention.

The third thing speakers at the conference emphasized was giving the brain something new to digest. This means learning something new or learning new responses to old problems. One of the experiments that supported this concept involved people who were going to take the test to be a London taxi driver. To pass the test, would-be drivers had to memorize every street in downtown London. Researchers decided to measure the hippocampus of a person before they started studying for the test and again after they passed the test. The hippocampus has an important role in memory. Researchers wanted to see what effect learning something new had on that part of the brain.

They found that instead of shrinking, as most of our hippocampi do with age, the hippocampi of those who passed the test had grown larger. And as a result, they didn't have any trouble with memory.

As we age, the hippocampus shrinks, which is why we become forgetful. The next time you can't remember something, blame it on your hippocampus.

I think I have a young brain, especially when it comes to memory. I attribute it to how I make goals for the New Year. One of my categories, intellectual goals, involves identifying new things I want to learn during the year. For several years, I wanted to learn Photoshop, which I did a little.

> **The next time you can't remember something, blame it on your hippocampus.**

For several other years, I wanted to learn to play the oboe, which I didn't do. Recently, I wanted to learn more about the Old Testament prophets, which I did. My point is that, whether I succeeded or failed, I at least tried. I was always learning something new. And my hippocampus thanked me.

Sometimes life throws us a curve, and we need to learn something new in order to solve a major life problem. That was certainly true for David as he tried to escape from Saul. We must have an open stance toward life and continually want to learn new things about current life problems and how to approach them.

A Man after God's Own Heart

The most familiar story about David is his confident confrontation of the Philistine giant named Goliath. This little guy who couldn't fit into King Saul's armor faced the fearsome giant with only a slingshot and five stones—and with a strong belief that no one should "defy the armies of the living God" (1 Sam. 17:26). He carried this conviction with him throughout his life.

We may also be familiar with the account of how Samuel went to Jesse's family to anoint the next king. None of Jesse's sons were God's choice, and that left Samuel confused. He asked if there were any other sons, and Jesse remembered that he had a son who was out in the fields taking care of the sheep. David's father had forgotten about him. How strange! It was an interesting family dynamic.

In the Psalms, we get a taste of the terror David faced during the years when King Saul hunted David with the intent to kill him. Saul knew that Samuel had already anointed David as the next king, and Saul was determined that there would be no King David in the future. Yet David was loyal to Saul, and even though he had two opportunities to kill Saul, he refused to do so. He would not lay hands on God's anointed one.

Unlike in other nations, Israel's throne was not inherited. Yet after Saul's death, his followers assumed that Saul's eldest son, Ishbosheth, would be the next king. In fact, he was crowned king in Israel and ruled for two years. Abner, Saul's faithful general, helped make that happen out of loyalty to Saul.

This was counter to what God wanted and expected. David was God's choice, and David knew that, for Samuel had anointed him king by God's will. But David had to proceed cautiously. And he did. One by one, the opposition went away. In 2 Samuel 1–4, we see what a shrewd and powerful leader David was becoming as these claimants to the throne were eliminated while he himself remained innocent of any involvement. As David waited, he "became stronger and stronger, while Saul's dynasty became weaker and weaker" (2 Sam. 3:1).

Before Samuel died, the prophet-priest had confronted Saul and told him, "You have not kept the command the LORD your God gave you. Had you kept it, the LORD would have established your kingdom over Israel forever. But now your kingdom must end, for the LORD has sought out a man after his own heart. The LORD has already appointed him to be the leader of his people,

because you have not kept the LORD's command"
(1 Sam. 13:13–14).

When the apostle Paul preached in Antioch of
Pisidia, he quoted Samuel's words to Saul: "But
God removed Saul and replaced him with David,
a man about whom God said, 'I have found David
son of Jesse, a man after my own heart. He will do
everything I want him to do'" (Acts 13:22).

The Dark Side of David

There was a dark side to David that is hard to rec-
oncile with his being a man after God's own heart.
But because David had a teachable heart, he was
able to learn from his mistakes.

Perhaps the most devastating thing that David
allowed to happen while he was running from
Saul involved the priest Ahimelech (see 1 Sam.
21–22). David told Ahimelech that Saul had sent
him on a private matter. David asked Ahimelech
for food and was given the only food the priest
had, the Bread of the Presence. This was the holy
bread that was placed before the Lord in the tab-
ernacle and was reserved for only the priests to
eat. Then David asked for a weapon, and Ahimelech gave him Goliath's sword. Ahimelech saw
no problem with what he was doing, especially

since David said he was on a mission for the king. David saw Doeg, Saul's chief herdsman, observing all this, but David did nothing about Doeg, even though he had to know that Doeg would tell everything to Saul, who would take revenge.

Doeg told Saul what had happened, and Saul sent for Ahimelech and his family. Ahimelech tried to tell Saul what he had done and why, but Saul wouldn't hear any of his explanations or defense. In his rage, Saul told his men to kill Ahimelech and his family. Saul's request was so outrageous that his men refused to carry out the order. So Saul turned to Doeg and said, "You do it." That day eighty-five priests were slaughtered by Doeg, each "still wearing their priestly garments. Then he went to Nob, the town of the priests, and killed the priests' families—men and women, children and babies—and all the cattle, donkeys, sheep, and goats" (1 Sam. 22:18–19). One man escaped and reported to David all that had happened. David said, "I knew it!" and he took full responsibility for what had happened (22:22). David had the capacity to confront and acknowledge his mistakes. Learning from his mistakes was part of the strength of his character.

But we haven't seen David at his worst. Second Samuel 11 recounts David's affair with Bathsheba and his murder of her husband, Uriah.

When David slept with Bathsheba, the unthinkable happened—she became pregnant. David thought of an easy solution—get her husband to come home and sleep with her. But Uriah would not go home and sleep with his wife while the rest of the soldiers were living in tents. David saw no other option but to eliminate Uriah to cover up his sin. No one would ever need to know the truth. Except the Lord already knew. The text simply says, "The LORD was displeased with what David had done. So the LORD sent Nathan the prophet to tell David this story" (2 Sam. 11:27–12:1).

> **David had the capacity to confront and acknowledge his mistakes. Learning from his mistakes was part of the strength of his character.**

Nathan told David about a rich man who owned many sheep and about a poor man who had only one lamb. The little lamb was like a family pet. When guests arrived at the rich man's house, the rich man did not want to slaughter one of his own sheep, so he took the poor man's little lamb and killed it and fed it to his guests.

When David heard the story, he was furious! He said the rich man deserved to die and had to repay the poor man four times what he had taken. "Then Nathan said to David, 'You are that man!'" (2 Sam. 12:7). Nathan went on to tell David all that he had done with Bathsheba and Uriah. When David heard this, he confessed to Nathan, "I have sinned against the LORD" (12:13).

Saul versus David

I have always been fascinated by a comparison of David and Saul. In many ways, at least humanly speaking, Saul was a better man than David. Saul was apparently a good father. His sons were loyal to him, even to the death. Jonathan was at his father's side in battle, and they died together. David's son Absalom led a rebellion against his father.

Saul was obedient to God and as the king had only one wife (Deut. 17:17), whereas David had at least eight wives, plus countless concubines. David gave in to the cultural expectations of a king, and in this way, David was like all the other kings of his day.

So why was David a man after God's own heart? I think in part it was because of the way he repented. He simply admitted his sin. David, in his encounter with Nathan, learned how to repent. David later penned Psalm 51 as an expression of his repentance.

> Have mercy on me, O God,
> because of your unfailing love.
> Because of your great compassion,
> blot out the stain of my sins.
> Wash me clean from my guilt.
> Purify me from my sin.
> For I recognize my rebellion;
> it haunts me day and night.
> Against you, and you alone, have I sinned;
> I have done what is evil in your sight.
> You will be proved right in what you say,
> and your judgment against me is just.
> (vv. 1–4)

When Samuel confronted Saul about disobeying God and not destroying the entire Amalekite nation, Saul quickly went on the defensive, claiming he had been obedient, even though he hadn't been. When he finally did admit his sin, he gave an excuse, claiming he had been afraid of the people and had done what they demanded. In the end, he was more concerned with what the people thought of him than repenting before God. He said, "I know I have sinned. But please, at least honor me before the elders of my people and before Israel by coming back with me so that I may worship the LORD your God" (1 Sam. 15:30).

Saul was worried about what the people would think of him. David was concerned about one thing—his relationship with the Lord. Throughout his life, in most situations, David was concerned with what God wanted in that situation.

Saul was worried about what the people would think of him. David was concerned about one thing—his relationship with the Lord.

That concern gave him a tender heart in his relationship with God—a heart that God could access.

David sinned, as we all do, but in contrast to Saul, David knew how to get his heart back in tune with God's heart. That's why God could say that David was a man after his own heart. Their hearts connected. In God's economy, it is not the sinning as much as it is the repenting that matters. God knows we're going to sin. He has solved the sin problem. He is concerned about our repentance. He wants us to have a teachable heart. A heart that knows how to repent is a heart after God's own heart.

A Question of Priorities

When Jan and I got married, I started working full-time and attending college part-time. For several years, I worked as a teller in a bank and continued to do that until I took a ministry position with Youth for Christ. I don't remember if every new person on staff was required to attend a two-week training session in Kansas City, but I attended.

The two weeks went by quickly, as each day was full of information regarding some aspect of the ministry. The man who was the director of the program in Kansas City led many of the sessions, and one thing he said made a deep impression on me. He paused in the middle of a session and seemingly out of the blue said, "Men, you are now married to the ministry!" This was a common understanding of the role ministry played in a Christian leader's life in the late 1950s, so I didn't question it—I simply accepted that it was true.

I was not only dumb enough to believe it but also naive enough to tell Jan. Her response was classic. She simply said, "Oh, I thought you were married to me." That simple, naive statement of mine took me almost eight years to unwind. I had a lot to learn.

Jan and I often referred to the first ten years of our marriage as having lived through "the great tribulation." It was a miracle we stayed together. And looking back, I am convinced that many of our problems were due to my attitude of being married to the ministry.

Skip ahead to the end of those ten years. We were the high school and college ministers at a church in Northern California. We had three boys, and life together was difficult. Just about every week I would go to a church that had a gym where a bunch of pastors would play basketball. Ron Ritchie was on the staff of that church. He and I typically skipped lunch with the other pastors and ate our bag lunches in his office, where we could talk. One conversation turned to my marital stress, and eventually I said something about being married to the ministry. Ron was appalled and spent the next weeks showing me from the Bible how I was wrong. My first priority was my wife, then my kids, and then my ministry. It took a while, but gradually it started to sink in.

On the day I changed my priorities, my marriage changed!

Science tells us that our brains can learn new things even as we age. If we combine that ability with a teachable heart, we can learn how to repent, we can learn how to fix a relationship, and we can learn how to adapt to life's challenges—we can learn new things that will help us live strong and finish well.

TO *Think* ABOUT, *Talk* ABOUT, AND *Pray* ABOUT

1. In what ways do we learn more from our failures than from our successes?
2. What do you think God meant when he said that David was a "man after his own heart"?
3. What can you learn from David about repentance?
4. What things can you learn at your age to help you finish well?

seven

FRIENDSHIP

I no longer call you servants, because a servant does not know his master's business. Instead, I have called you friends, for everything that I learned from my Father I have made known to you.

JOHN 15:15 NIV

We are wired in such a way that we are meant to connect with other people. If you're a man, you may disagree. But there is evidence that the statement is true.

Studies show that women live longer than men, in part because they refuse to live life alone. The same studies show that married men live longer than single men. But if a single man has a pet, it's the great equalizer. He lives just as long as a married man. That's the way it is—we're just not meant to go it alone.

That's a truth Solomon was seeking to express when he wrote, "Two people are better off than one, for they can help each other succeed. If one person falls, the other can reach out and help. But someone who falls alone is in real trouble. Likewise, two people lying close together can keep each other warm. But how can one be warm alone? A person standing alone can be attacked and defeated, but two can stand back-to-back and conquer. Three are even better, for a triple-braided cord is not easily broken" (Eccles. 4:9–12).

It's natural for people to connect with other people. Most women live for connection; most men agree in principle but would rather go it alone.

Why are men loners? I say it all begins on the playground. Watch an elementary school playground during recess. The girls tend to sit in clusters—talking with one another, learning how to relate. Most of the boys play a competitive game. Oh, some of the girls play the game and enjoy the competition, and a few of the boys would rather talk, but that's not how they tend to divide.

Perhaps men are loners because of our childhood heroes. In my day, men were portrayed as strong when they were alone. One of my heroes growing up was the Lone Ranger. I couldn't wait for the show to come on. The Lone Ranger and his trusted companion, Tonto, could solve any problem. And as the program ended, they would ride off into the sunset with a voice saying, "Who was that masked man?" The truth was the Lone Ranger was never alone—there were always two of them. Somehow I missed that one.

David's relationship with Jonathan often makes men uncomfortable. But David discovered that the strength of a man's character is related to his ability to connect deeply with other men in his life. Unfortunately, many men today don't know how to have deep friendships with other men. They don't even have another man they can rely on to be accountable to. They can talk sports or the stock market, but to talk about heart matters— that's not masculine. As a result, when a man struggles, he typically struggles alone. He has no male friends on whom he can depend.

> "Two people are better off than one, for they can help each other succeed. . . . Three are even better, for a triple-braided cord is not easily broken." (Eccles. 4:9, 12)

For David, the depth of his friendship with Jonathan was the key to their success as men. There was no going it alone for either of them. This is a lesson every man needs to learn. Men need to become comfortable with healthy relationships with other men.

Maybe boys growing up today will be influenced by new male characters, like those in the Marvel movies, who realize they are stronger when they are with others rather than alone.

Servants or Slaves and Friends

Imagine you are sitting in the upper room with the disciples. Jesus has washed your feet, and you have shared the Passover meal together. Jesus starts talking about loving one another and then says, "I no longer call you slaves" (John 15:15). It's important to understand that being called a slave—or as some translations prefer, a servant—wasn't an insult, nor was it something to be ashamed of. Moses was called a "servant of God" (Deut. 34:5), and so were Joshua (Josh. 24:29) and David (Ps. 89:20). Paul felt honored to use the title "a slave of God" (Titus 1:1), as did James (James 1:1). But in John 15, Jesus has something better for the disciples, and he expresses it by calling them friends.

At that time in the Roman Empire, much had been written about friendship, but the way people defined friendship was limited. It could be experienced only by people of the same sex, the same social class, and the same tribal group. Friendship with social inferiors wasn't possible. People typically viewed friendship in practical terms. There had to be a mutual advantage for both parties, like having someone who would pick you up after the boat docked.

What did it mean for the disciples when Jesus called them friends? In the Old Testament, only Abraham was called a friend of God (Isa. 41:8). But now, being a friend of Jesus meant you were a friend of God. To understand how incredible this was, we need to consider a custom in the court of the Roman emperor and in the courts of many Eastern kings. A select group of men were called friends of the emperor or friends of the king. These men had unlimited access to the emperor or king—at any time! They had the closest, most intimate connection with the emperor or king and were able to go and talk to the emperor or king at any time. They were consulted first. They were the first to know what was going on in the mind of the emperor or king.

Jesus calls us to be his friends, and therefore we are also called to be friends of God. That has tremendous implications for us. First, we are no longer treated as servants/slaves. Now we are in the know. That in itself is a tremendous honor.

> **Jesus calls us to be his friends, and therefore we are also called to be friends of God.**

Second, we have the right to enter into God's presence. Being a friend of God means we have access to God. By calling us friends, Jesus did an amazing thing. He gave us intimacy with God so that God is no longer a distant stranger; he is our intimate friend.

> **Being a friend of God means we have access to God. God is no longer a distant stranger; he is our intimate friend.**

Third, as friends of Jesus, we are his partners. Jesus has given us the honor of being partners with him in his mission. He has shared his plans with us. We know why he came. We know what he wants us to do before his return.

We have a choice to make. We can be Jesus's friend, or we can refuse his incredible offer.

What Kind of Friend

Friendship means various things today. We have "friends" on Facebook we've never met. We have friends who are just acquaintances. We know each other, but there's no consistent, ongoing relationship. It comes and goes. We have friends who are happy to run us to the airport or to pick us up. They know we would do the same for them. Some of us may even have friends who share the depths of their hearts with us and who will listen to our hearts in response. Those kinds of friends are becoming harder to find.

Barring any major changes, our relationship patterns are pretty well set by the time we hit midlife. Ask yourself, "Do I have friends with whom I share my dreams, my disappointments, my fears, my longings, and my struggles? How often do we share these things with each other?" I wonder how many of us have that kind of friend.

When Jesus made the disciples his friends, he also made us his friends. That means you are a friend of God. I am a friend of God. But how often do we marvel at the reality of our ability to enter God's presence at any time? How often do we even contemplate that incredible reality? Not often enough, I would venture to say. Perhaps we have no human context by which we can experience it.

First John 4:20 states, "If someone says, 'I love God,' but hates a fellow believer, that person is a liar; for if we don't love people we can see, how can we love God, whom we cannot see?" If I can't experience something with people, whom I can see, then how can I experience it with the invisible God? If I can't experience openness with a friend, and know what that feels like, then how

We experience friendship with God to the degree we are able to be friends with fellow believers.

can I experience it with God? On the other hand, if I can't wait to share something exciting with a friend, then I probably know what it's like to want to share something exciting with God. We experience friendship with God to the degree we are able to be friends with fellow believers.

Spiritual Friendship

Jesus laid down his life for humanity. Many of his followers in those early years laid down their lives for the faith. For many years, I wondered if the apostle Paul knew that this was his destiny—to die alone. But then I looked at how he conducted his ministry. I remembered that Barnabas accompanied him on his first missionary journey. Silas accompanied him on his second missionary journey. Paul's friendships with his coworkers in the gospel not only shaped his ministry but also added to my understanding of how his idea of spiritual friendship was different from the secular idea of the day regarding friendship.

I was surprised when someone pointed out that most of Paul's letters include the names of coauthors. I had always believed, based on the assumption that Paul's eyes were bad, that they were just taking dictation. Instead of envisioning a solitary Paul sitting thoughtfully at a desk, we might do better to imagine the Holy Spirit inspiring him in his tent-making shop as he wrote to the Thessalonians and Corinthians, with advice and suggestions from Timothy, Sosthenes, and Silas (1 Cor. 1:1; 2 Cor. 1:1; 1 Thess. 1:1; 2 Thess. 1:1). Or we could visualize Paul talking things over with Aristarchus in a prison cell and then whispering through the keyhole of a prison door ideas he wanted Timothy to record for the Colossians (Col. 1:1; 4:10).[1]

Paul also referred to people who were helping him in his ministry. The first sixteen verses of the final chapter of Romans list the people he wanted readers to greet. He called them "coworkers," "brother," "sister," and "dear friend." He frequently talked about the deep affection he had for his readers. This was especially true in the letter he wrote to the Philippians. He wasn't afraid to express his care and concern for the churches and for individuals in the various churches.

1. Michael F. Bird, "St. Paul Among Friends," *Christian History* 132 (2019): 7, https://christianhistoryinstitute.org/magazine/article/st-paul-among-friends.

Paul's letters had to be delivered to far-off congregations, and he wanted to make sure his instructions were followed. Timothy, Titus, Phoebe, Tychicus, Epaphroditus, Epaphras, and others were trusted by Paul to implement the instructions his letters contained. For example, Paul commended Timothy to the Corinthians: "For this reason I have sent to you Timothy, my son whom I love, who is faithful in the Lord. He will remind you of my way of life in Christ Jesus, which agrees with what I teach everywhere in every church" (1 Cor. 4:17 NIV).

The apostle Paul took friendship to a whole new level. Perhaps we should call it *spiritual friendship*. This recognizes that there are added dimensions when friendship is infused with Christianity. Jesus's exhortation to love one another wasn't just an add-on or an afterthought. It was an essential part of true friendship. There is genuine love and affection for one another. As you read through the list in Romans 16, you can feel the connection between Paul and the people he lists. Paul transformed the secular model of friendship into something deeper and more lasting.

The added dimensions include the idea that friends bring one another closer to Christ. They lovingly hold one another accountable for spiritual growth. Paul instructs his readers, "Don't just pretend to love others. Really love them. Hate what is wrong. Hold tightly to what is good. Love each other with genuine affection, and take delight in honoring each other" (Rom. 12:9–10).

Building Spiritual Friendships

Over thirty-five years ago, a woman at our church in Northern California decided to get some women together for a weekend retreat. The women had a great time, and at the end of the weekend, someone wondered out loud whether the husbands would be open to joining them for a weekend. Someone said, "Let's just do it. Let's plan it and assume they will participate."

So our group, which we called "D'tenuvus," was born. We called our group that because it was made up of ten people. For over thirty years, we met twice a year for long weekends. Three members of the group have died, and we haven't met the last couple years due to our increasing physical limitations. But we keep in touch regularly.

We met in some interesting places—from beach houses to mountain cabins—plus we took two cruises together. During weekend gatherings, we shared what was going on in our lives. Then we all prayed for each family.

If you have been reading this chapter and realize you don't have any close friends, is there any hope? Yes, there is hope, but building spiritual friendships will take some work.

I asked my wife how she would help me find spiritual friends. Even though I told her it was a hypothetical question for this book, she started coming up with a list of names. It was a good list. So you can begin identifying possible friends by having a conversation with your spouse or a family member who knows you well. If you are not comfortable talking to your spouse or a family member, maybe you can talk to your pastor. Try to identify three or four potential spiritual friends.

As you go about this process, it's important for you to be in prayer, as you want God's guidance in what you're doing. Ask God to give you a sense of which person you should approach first.

Set up a breakfast or a lunch with the person you're going to approach first. As you talk together, at some point share with the person that you are looking for a spiritual friend. Talk about why you feel it is important for you to have a friend who holds you spiritually accountable and keeps you anticipating the joys of life as you age. Ask if they might be open to pursuing such a friendship with you. If they aren't, respect their decision and consider the next person you want to approach. If they are, don't rush the process. You are getting to know someone at a deeper level and letting them get to know you at a deeper level. That's your only agenda. In subsequent meetings, talk about your faith. Talk about your dreams— what you hoped life would be like at this point in time. Talk about your disappointments. Use discernment but stay open to allowing the relationship to develop long-term. If you don't click, don't worry. If one or both of you want to part ways, the time was still well spent, and you can continue your search.

If you *do* click, set up a schedule for when you're going to meet. I suggest meeting at least twice a month. It is important that you make a commitment to meet regularly. There will be times when you will be too tired to meet, but meet anyway. There will be times when you won't want to meet because of the missteps you're making in your life, but those are the times you especially need a spiritual friend.

A Friendship

It's interesting how deep friendships develop. I've been trying to understand how my friendship with Steve Arterburn developed. I've looked back over nearly forty years of friendship and collaboration on a number of projects. It seems like our friendship just happened. Maybe that's the way most friendships begin. They just happen. It's what you do after a friendship starts that makes it a deep friendship.

Steve and I met as part of the leadership of a relatively new church. Steve was involved with the music ministry, and I was involved with adult education. I remember asking Steve to teach a course on the topic "that Christian sitting next to you could be an alcoholic." It was a great success. We hit it off, and our friendship began. It only seemed natural that we would write a book together, and we've written many of them since then. One of the first we wrote was titled *The Angry Man*. It released the same time as John Townsend and Henry Cloud's book *Boundaries*. They sold millions of copies, and we jokingly said we sold eight copies.

Steve and I were competitors in mental health inpatient treatment programs. Steve started New

Life Treatment Centers, and I was a partner in the Minirth-Meier Clinic West. I don't think we ever talked business, and maybe that's why our friendship continued to grow during the time when we were business competitors.

What may have sealed our friendship was a joint project that didn't start out as a joint project. Unbeknownst to both of us, we were each working on a proposal for a Twelve Steps Bible. Steve turned in a proposal to one person at Tyndale House; my agent turned in my proposal to someone else there. The publication committee met to discuss the possibility of doing a Twelve Steps Bible and eventually said, "Yes, let's do it." That led to someone asking, "Who's going to call Dave?" Then someone else asked, "Why call Dave? Who's going to call Steve?" For the first time they realized they were talking about two different proposals from two different people. Someone asked if maybe we would work together, and when the publisher suggested it to us, we both said yes. The product ended up far better than what either one of us would have produced separately.

Neither one of us—and especially the publisher—had any idea how successful a project like that Bible would be. Now, with close to four million copies sold, it's easy to see how our work was cut out for us.

Steve likes to say we have survived as friends all these years because we both worked the Twelve Steps. I think he's right.

Friendships take work, and deep friendships—spiritual friendships—take a willingness to be especially open and honest about our lives. But the work we put into our friendships reaps benefits in helping us live strong so we can finish well.

TO *Think* ABOUT, *Talk* ABOUT, AND *Pray* ABOUT

1. How would you define a spiritual friendship?
2. On a scale of 1 to 10, with 10 being very comfortable and 1 being very uncomfortable, how comfortable are you with having spiritual friendships? Why? What makes you uncomfortable? What makes you comfortable?
3. Who are, or could be, your spiritual friends?

eight

RESILIENCE

The godly may trip seven times,
but they will get up again.
But one disaster is enough to
overthrow the wicked.

PROVERBS 24:16

Let's start with a definition of *resilience* so we are on the same page. Resilience is the process of adapting well when we are faced with adversity, trauma, tragedy, threats, or significant sources of stress, including such things as family and relationship problems, serious health problems, workplace problems, and financial problems.

You know the feeling—what starts as a day filled with fun winds up going sideways at every turn. As you get in your car to head to your son's house to pick up your granddaughter for a big pancake breakfast at IHOP, he calls and delivers the bad news that she disobeyed her mom and needs to face some consequences (not seeing you). Well, that takes a cute Facebook post off the table. Since you're still hungry, you pull into your favorite diner. Just as your food is delivered, your wife calls to tell you that the next-door neighbor fell and she's following the ambulance to the hospital. You'll have to get (or make) lunch and dinner for yourself . . . and you should stay on call in case the husband needs anything.

Game. Set. Match.

No granddaughter, no time to go hit balls at the range—and bad nutrition to top it off. This day will test your ability to be resilient.

Although you won't think about it at the time, your response to these stressors can actually hone your ability to become even more resilient and empower you to grow and improve your life. The growth comes as you learn to cope when life throws you a curve. Resilience is more than just simply surviving adversity. Resilience is the ability to bounce back while learning additional skills so you're even more ready to bounce back in the next crisis.

Resilience is the ability to bounce back while learning additional skills so you're even more ready to bounce back in the next crisis.

While some individuals may appear to be more resilient than others, resilience is not a personality trait that only some people possess. I remember my earliest exposure to the concept of resilience. The research at that time focused on children, and some children were labeled resilient, while other children were labeled not resilient. Further research indicated that children considered not resilient were probably wounded emotionally in some way that blocked their natural ability in the area of resilience. The truth is that resilience involves behaviors and thoughts that anyone can learn and develop. Resilience is

Resilience is ordinary, not extraordinary.

ordinary, not extraordinary. That's good news for those of us who are weak in the area of resilience.

Resilience and Faith

Jesus warned the disciples about what was coming in their lives. In the upper room after the Passover supper was finished, he said, "I have told you these things so that you won't abandon your faith. For you will be expelled from the synagogues, and the time is coming when those who kill you will think they are doing a holy service for God. This is because they have never known the Father or me. Yes, I'm telling you these things now, so that when they happen, you will remember my warning" (John 16:1–4). The disciples would have many opportunities to develop a healthy resilience. The same is true for Christians today.

When someone becomes a believer, life becomes more complicated. The enemy wants to cause us to abandon our faith. In reality, though, the enemy is giving us the opportunity to develop our resilience. What are we going to learn this time around that helps us hold on to our faith?

Each person has their own way of developing resilience. Joseph was hated by his brothers, played the favorite with his mother and father, and dreamed what seemed to be extremely egocentric dreams. He was sold into slavery by his brothers, taken to Egypt—a strange land with a strange language—and sold to Potiphar, the captain of the guard in Pharaoh's court. He was later falsely accused of rape by his master's wife, and was imprisoned and seemingly forgotten. Through it all, Joseph quietly reaffirmed his faith regardless of the circumstances. He continued to rely on God and refused to give up. Even in prison, he was put in charge of all the other prisoners.

Moses started out life not knowing where his loyalty belonged, whether he was Jewish or Egyptian. When word reached Pharaoh that Moses had killed an Egyptian man, Moses fled Egypt and ended up living in the land of Midian. He was forty years old when he fled, and he lived for forty more years before God called him to a task that would teach him much about resilience.

There was a new pharaoh on the throne, and God told Moses to go to him and secure the release of the people of Israel from bondage. Moses doubted his abilities, and eventually God gave him his brother, Aaron, to speak for him. The first time Moses and Aaron went to see Pharaoh, their appeals fell on deaf ears and resulted in more labor with fewer resources. Even the people of Israel refused to listen to the promise of deliverance. God sent Moses and Aaron to speak to Pharaoh again, but Pharaoh's heart was hardened. Eventually, God sent ten plagues. Only after the tenth plague, the death of every firstborn in the land, did Pharaoh relent and free the Israelites. But after they were freed, the people of Israel complained about how much better everything was back in Egypt. Finally, Moses got fed up and complained to God about the people and their demands.

> And Moses said to the LORD, "Why are you treating me, your servant, so harshly? Have mercy on me! What did I do to deserve the burden of all these people? Did I give birth to them? Did I bring them into the world? Why did you

tell me to carry them in my arms like a mother carries a nursing baby? How can I carry them to the land you swore to give their ancestors? Where am I supposed to get meat for all these people? They keep whining to me, saying, 'Give us meat to eat!' I can't carry all these people by myself! The load is far too heavy!" (Num. 11:11–14)

God told Moses to pick seventy men; they would help him bear the burden of the people. Then the Lord gave them meat in the form of quail.

Moses often reacted to a situation before learning a new response, but he kept learning new things about leadership, about staying on task, and about being honest with the Lord. He too learned to be resilient.

The obvious example of resilience from the New Testament is the apostle Paul. In 2 Corinthians 11, Paul shares what he has been through.

I have worked harder, been put in prison more often, been whipped times without number, and faced death again and again. Five different times the Jewish leaders gave me thirty-nine lashes. Three times I was beaten with rods. Once I was stoned. Three times I was shipwrecked. Once I spent a whole night and a day adrift at sea. I have traveled on many long journeys. I have faced danger from rivers and from robbers. I have faced danger from my own people, the Jews, as well as from the Gentiles. I have faced danger in the cities, in the deserts, and on the seas. And I have faced danger from men who claim to be believers but are not. I have worked hard and long, enduring many sleepless nights. I have been hungry and thirsty and have often gone without food. I have shivered in the cold, without enough clothing to keep me warm. (vv. 23–27)

Paul's resilience enabled him to be undeterred from his mission regardless of the opposition.

The key is that you learn new skills in difficult times to build your resilience and keep the faith.

Whether you are the silent "put up with it" type like Joseph and Paul or a complainer like Moses, the key is that you learn new skills in difficult times to build your resilience and keep the faith.

How to Increase Your Resilience

How do you increase your resilience? Well, what do you do when you want to increase the size of a muscle? Let's say you want to build the size of your upper arms and increase the strength of those muscles. First, you have to recognize that building strength is going to take time. Your muscles will not become stronger overnight. And then you have to be intentional. You have to make it your intention to work on developing those muscles.

The same ideas apply if you want to become more resilient when facing the pressures of life. Getting through pain and disappointment isn't necessarily easy. But the more you develop the skills you need to carry on after the death of a loved one, a job loss, or another setback, the more equipped you will be to live life strong and finish well.

Begin by working on building connections with empathetic and understanding people who will validate your feelings. When your resilience is running low, resist the tendency to isolate yourself. You need to be around people who care about you. You may need to join a support group of other people who are working on similar issues.

> **When your resilience is running low, resist the tendency to isolate yourself.**

Take care of your body. Self-care is an important practice for mental health and building resilience. Stress is just as much physical as it is emotional. Positive lifestyle choices such as proper nutrition, ample sleep, hydration, and regular exercise strengthen your body and mind so you are better able to handle stress, anxiety, and depression. Resist negative outlets. You may be tempted to use alcohol or drugs to numb the pain. Instead, focus on managing stress rather than trying to eliminate the feeling of stress.

Make time for spiritual practices such as prayer and Bible study. When stress builds, read passages that remind you that God is with you, and take your concerns to him in prayer. Don't let the pain of your personal trial cause you to abandon spiritual disciplines in your life.

Find a way to help others. You can volunteer with a local homeless shelter or support a friend in their own time of need. When you help others, you find a sense of purpose, foster self-worth, and connect with other people, all of which can empower you to grow in resilience.

Brainstorm with a friend about what you can do about a specific problem in your life. Ask yourself questions like these: Am I part of the problem? Do I have a tendency to blame others? Do I demand perfection, or am I able to accept that life is a mix of losses and wins? Attempt to identify contributing factors that are specific, temporary, and personal. Then come up with some steps you can take to address these factors. Try to see the problem as an opportunity for self-discovery and self-improvement.

Try to maintain a positive attitude. A positive attitude tempers the impact both on the mind and the body when the pressure builds. It also helps you avoid irrational forms of thinking, such as catastrophizing or thinking the worst about a situation. Such thinking eliminates any possible options that might be productive.

Learn from your past experiences, good and bad. Remembering how you handled a situation successfully may help you identify factors that led to your success and give you confidence going forward. Then you can look for ways to apply your past successes to your current stressors. You can also learn from your failures. Failing at something is a common human experience. Statistics show that everyone, regardless of background or skills, will fail at something important at least once in their lifetime. That doesn't make it any easier to accept a failure, but learning to be okay with making mistakes, whether big or small, is a part of developing resilience. Explore why things went wrong in the past and make a plan for what you can do in the future.

Practice developing resilience so that when the next stressor hits, you are better prepared to face it. Being resilient is a part of living strong so you can finish well.

TO *Think* ABOUT, *Talk* ABOUT, AND *Pray* ABOUT

1. Before reading this chapter, how would you have defined resilience? How has your definition changed?
2. Describe some of the lessons you have learned in your life.
3. What steps can you take to become more resilient?

nine

A LIFE REVIEW

Remember the wonders he has performed,
his miracles, and the rulings he has
given.

1 CHRONICLES 16:12

an and I were sitting and talking together in our home office. Eventually, the discussion turned to the five men I've talked about in this book, the men I've known who have impacted my life.

"Why just five?" she asked. "What about . . . ?" and then she named several people who are close friends.

"It wasn't about our friendship," I responded. "It was that they were there at a critical point in my life, and they had an impact on the direction my life took as a result of our interaction. I guess I was doing a life review without even knowing that's what I was doing.

"I think it started when I thought of David Engstrom, and as I was remembering my relationship with him, I thought about how he had impacted my life at a critical stage of my development. That took me on a search of my memory to see who else had a similar effect on the direction of my life."

"What's a life review?" Jan asked. I had to admit I didn't really know, and that sent us both to a search of the internet.

A Life Review

The concept of a life review was identified by gerontologist Robert Butler in the 1960s. He saw it as something that typically happens spontaneously as people grow older. A more structured form of a life review was developed some years later and is called a guided autobiography. The purpose of a life review, whether structured or not, is to recall and evaluate positive and negative memories. It involves linking memories together in order to come to a sense of wholeness and completion about the life we have lived.

There are many benefits to doing a life review. It helps us deal with unresolved issues in our life, helps us reevaluate the deeper sense of meaning and purpose in our life, enhances our psychological well-being, deepens the store of wisdom we already possess, and enriches what we have to share with others.

Sometimes a life review can be painful, especially for someone who believes they have committed unforgivable

> A life review helps us deal with unresolved issues and reevaluate the deeper sense of meaning and purpose in our life.

acts or who is unable to forgive someone from the past who has hurt them. For others, this process can bring painful memories to the surface so they can be dealt with. If someone has experienced a traumatic event, post-traumatic stress disorder may make it difficult for them to do this process alone. If your memories are overwhelming, you may want to consider working with a therapist either individually or in a group setting. This will be one of the best—and perhaps one of the hardest—things you do. You're stepping onto the road toward healing, and how long that road becomes is largely up to you.

Looking back at old conflicts in our lives and considering what happened can help us find closure. Reviewing past experiences from a more mature point of view can lead to a less conflicted perception of the situation. This is especially true when the conflict involved a family member who isn't present when we are reminiscing. There is a freedom in reminiscing that allows us the ability to change our point of view.

Memories

Memories typically come uninvited and point to something important. They come in the service of wholeness and well-being. Each memory and the emotions it evokes provide an opportunity for us to better understand ourselves and our life. Revisiting the people and scenes of the past that come calling allows us to savor and be grateful for the blessings we have known.

Talking with family members about our memories helps preserve family history. Younger members of the family may not have been alive during the times we are remembering. Sharing these memories can bring a family closer together.

Memories provide an opportunity to better understand ourselves and our life.

Sharing the memory of a painful situation with someone can reduce stress. One reason is that it allows us to resolve issues from the past that we may not have dealt with before. We may have been holding on to negative emotions and probably didn't know how to deal with them. Getting that memory out in the open can pave the way for healing.

Sharing memories can also reduce symptoms of depression, even in people with early dementia. Reminiscing distracts them from worrying about their medical condition or their memory failures. It can also lower blood pressure and heart rate.

Uncomfortable memories are like nightmares and are also important to pay attention to because they illuminate the parts of our history that need to be reckoned with and integrated. Welcoming and reflecting on memories about which we still carry guilt or resentment can ultimately lead to necessary forgiveness, deeper understanding, and acceptance of ourselves and others.

Our memories may bring us face-to-face with our complexities and our contradictions. Paying attention to our contradictions may give us the richest understanding of ourselves. This is an essential part of the development of ego integrity.

> Paying attention to our contradictions may give us the richest understanding of ourselves.

How to Begin

Starting a life review may be as simple as paying attention to what you remember. When you have a memory, ask yourself some important questions such as "Why am I remembering this now?" and "Why is this memory important?" If you get some answers to these questions, ask yourself, "What is the purpose or meaning being expressed in this memory?" and "How does it relate to some of the other memories of this that I've had along the way?" By answering these questions, you are on your way to a life review.

If you're having difficulty getting started, try to wake up your memories. Look through old photographs, albums, or yearbooks. Look at photographs taken on family vacations. Seeing familiar places and faces may prompt memories and stories that you've long since forgotten.

Talk with somebody about movies that may have impacted you when you were young. Why not rent the movies and watch them again? Talk about the holidays when you were young. What do you remember the most? What was the best part of the holidays for you? Talk about the music you listened to. Did you go to any concerts? Talk about some of the items in your home that have special meaning to you. Why are they special to you?

Once you have the flow of memories started, you can begin the evaluating process. What are some of the common threads that run through your memories? What personal values do your memories represent? Who are the people who recur in your memories? Are they meaningful?

For example, I was thinking back to the summer after I graduated from high school. It was a chaotic summer filled with highlights—I met Jan and I also decided to follow Jesus. I remembered stuff from my senior year in high school, and then I remembered

What are some of the common threads that run through your memories? What personal values do your memories represent? Who are the people who recur in your memories?

my Sunday lunches with David Engstrom and the impact he had on my life. I wondered if there were other people like him who impacted my life at critical points, so I did a review of the people who were in my life and the events that took place in different locations.

I remembered how Jim Smoke got me involved in ministry, and how Bob Battles took me through an informal training to experience a variety of ways to do ministry. Ron Ritchie was clearly instrumental in my getting my marriage right, and Steve Arterburn taught me so much about the field of recovery and also influenced much of what we together have written and spoken on over the years.

I didn't do this in one sitting; I did it off and on over a period of about six months. When I finished—and I knew I was finished—I had identified the five men you have met in this book, and I knew more about myself and how I became the person I am. As I look back over the process I went through, I can say it was very beneficial.

Perhaps you want to do a life review so that you can relive your memories, deal with any unresolved issues or conflicts, gain a deeper appreciation for the blessings you've experienced, pass along your memories to the next generation—and finish well!

TO *Think* ABOUT, *Talk* ABOUT, AND *Pray* ABOUT

1. What appeals to you about doing a life review? What scares you about doing one?
2. If you want to do a life review but are having trouble remembering your past, what are some things you can do to jog your memories?

ten

THE GIFTS
OF AGING

The glory of the young is their
strength;
the gray hair of experience is the
splendor of the old.

PROVERBS 20:29

The key to aging well, and finishing well, is to accept that aging affects us. The aches and pains are part of the process we will each experience. So is the gray hair. But there are some special gifts reserved for those who embrace the process.

The Gift of the Present

For much of our lives, we focus on the future. When we're in school, we're looking ahead to graduation. When we get our first job, we think about how to get promoted or get a better job. We save for the future. When we have children, we focus on their future.

At some point, our thoughts for the future become focused on quality of life for our children and our grandchildren. We think less about our personal future. But we don't want to become locked in the past either. Those who become locked in the past end up in despair and depression, or guilt. Likewise, we do not want to get locked in a fearful but empty future.

The future belongs to God, and he can be trusted with it. The past is in the past, and hopefully we've done the work of resolving any painful parts of our past. That leaves us with the present. Ask God for the grace to live in the present and to look with hope to the future.

> **The future belongs to God, and he can be trusted with it.**

The Gift of Gratitude

Every day is a gift from God for which we can be thankful. As we age, we can see more and more that even the disappointments were a gift from God. Often we learn more from the disappointments than from the successes. Over time we can see how disappointments made us wiser and more mature. Those were the times when our faith grew, when prayer became more important, when qualities we didn't even know were in us emerged.

An attitude of gratitude has many benefits. People who daily exercise gratitude experience more positive emotions, are more likely to accomplish their goals, and report feeling more alert, energetic, and alive. They sleep better, have lower blood pressure, and live an average of seven to nine years longer. In addition, gratitude diverts attention away from stress and worry, brings closure to unresolved traumatic memories, and helps us be more connected to other people.

> **Every day is a gift from God for which we can be thankful.**

Why not start a gratitude journal? Take ten minutes at the end of each day to think of the people who helped you that day. Then focus on any feelings of gratitude they evoke. Make it a point the next day to express gratitude to someone about whom you felt gratitude. And ask God for the grace to be ever aware of the gift of gratitude and to be ever thankful.

The Gift of Letting Go

Major life changes such as retirement, children leaving the nest, and losses of various kinds often lead us to rethink what is necessary in our life. Moving out of a house that is now too big is an emotional decision for many. There is a kind of involuntary downsizing that comes from the physical limitations of aging, such as when we can no longer drive or climb stairs. None of this is easy. We may react with sadness, anger, or denial.

Take all those emotions to God, and ask him to give you what you need and the grace to let go of the rest.

When we rethink what is necessary and let go of the rest, we often find that our spiritual life is most important. There can be a spiritual ease that comes with age. Our soul has opened up to God more so that we live more in God's presence. It has become second nature. While the young are struggling to build the muscles of their souls, those who are practiced in the faith don't think about it anymore. As Paul said to the Corinthians, "That is why we never give up. Though our bodies are dying, our spirits are being renewed every day" (2 Cor. 4:16).

The saints among us are a source of spiritual power that often remains untapped. Whereas the young are seeking to find the reality of God, many gray-haired saints have walked in the reality of God for more than half a century. They have an important witness to share of what God can do, what he has done, and what he is doing in the world. With many years of experience, they know

The saints among us are a source of spiritual power that often remains untapped.

the power of prayer, the importance of worship, the value of personal ministry, and the validity of the Word of God. This knowledge takes years and years and years to gain. It needs to be written down. It has great value if it is shared and received.

The Gift of Wisdom

The gift of wisdom comes with gray hair. Wisdom is a product of many years of walking and talking with God. It can be gained only by sitting for a lifetime at the feet of Jesus and learning from him. The young can give us many things, but wisdom will never be one of them. Only the foolish believe in instant wisdom, instant knowledge, or instant discernment. True wisdom, knowledge, and discernment are God's gifts to the body of Christ through those who have given God time to season their lives.

> Wisdom is a product of many years of walking and talking with God.

Ecclesiastes 3:1 says, "To everything there is a season, a time for every purpose under heaven" (NKJV). Those who are well-aged have a purpose, and that purpose is too often neglected. They are a resource that is spiritually manifested toward the end of their mortal existence.

Older people have much to share with young people, but listening must come first. Listening opens the door to relationship. Young people suffer deeply from feeling they're not listened to, they're not seen as who they are. When an older person expresses genuine interest and doesn't immediately fall into advice mode, they can build relationship. That's step one.

Step two is modeling how we deal with failure. We can assure young people not to be afraid of it. Factoring failure into our story is not only honest but also reassuring. Most of us have learned so much more from failure than from our successes. When we fail, we stay up late at night chewing on things. That's when deep learning happens. Failure is a big teacher and is an important building block in gaining wisdom.

Age is the beginning of wisdom; it has lessons to be taught. The golden years may not seem golden to you if you are living them, but be generous and let others mine your gold, for as with all spiritual blessings, wisdom's value comes only when we give it away.

The Gift of Mortality

The older I get, the harder it is not to think about my mortality. I ignored the question of mortality until I was in my late fifties. It wasn't until I learned I had Parkinson's that I began to feel vulnerable—that my death was inevitable. But I have grown relatively comfortable with that reality, and the older I get, the more grateful I am for the time I have been given in this life. In fact, the more I accept my own mortality, the more comfortable I am with its reality.

Perhaps that was the thinking behind the Japanese samurai as each day they prepared for the reality that this could be the day they might die. Only then, when they were fully prepared to die, were they fully prepared to live. When we are prepared to die, we have a deeper appreciation for the gifts of life.

We each have had preparation for death through the little deaths we have experienced: the death of a dream, of a job, of a relationship. As we have gone through these little deaths in our lives,

> The more I accept my own mortality, the more comfortable I am with its reality.

our hearts have become less hardened and more tender. These deaths are more likely to break a heart open than to break it apart. These deaths have allowed us to exercise our hearts and to be prepared for death itself. Such preparation helps us to live fully until the day we die.

TO *Think* ABOUT, *Talk* ABOUT, AND *Pray* ABOUT

1. Which of the gifts of aging discussed in this chapter are you thankful for? Why?
2. What other gifts of aging can you think of?

Dr. David Stoop (1937–2021) was the founder and director of the Center for Family Therapy and cohost of the nationally syndicated *New Life Live!* radio and TV program. The author of more than thirty books, including *Forgiving What You'll Never Forget* and *Change Your Thoughts, Change Your Life*, David coauthored several books with his wife, Jan, and led seminars and retreats on topics such as marital relationships, parenting, men's issues, fathering, and forgiveness. Learn more at www.DrStoop.com.

More from **Dr. Stoop**

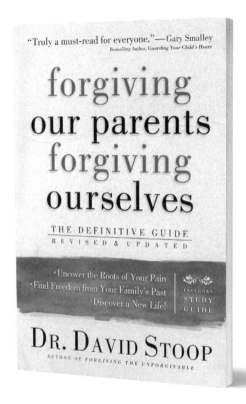

"Truly a must-read for everyone." —Gary Smalley
Bestselling Author, *Guarding Your Child's Heart*

forgiving
our parents
forgiving
ourselves

THE DEFINITIVE GUIDE
REVISED & UPDATED

- Uncover the Roots of Your Pain
- Find Freedom from Your Family's Past
- Discover a New Life!

INCLUDES
STUDY
GUIDE

DR. DAVID STOOP
AUTHOR OF *FORGIVING THE UNFORGIVABLE*

For more than fifteen years, people who grew up in dysfunctional families have found hope, healing, and the power to move forward with their lives in the classic *Forgiving Our Parents, Forgiving Ourselves*. Now, in this revised and updated edition, a new generation can move beyond failure to forgiveness by understanding the roots of their pain.

How do you forgive
the unforgivable?

Dr. David Stoop compassionately guides you down a biblical road from the pain of bitter hurt to the peace found only in heartfelt forgiveness, even for the worst of offenses. In doing so, he opens up the way for you to experience the freedom that forgiveness brings.

ATTITUDE IS EVERYTHING

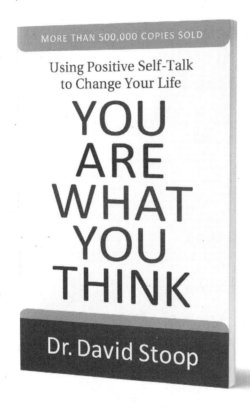

MORE THAN 500,000 COPIES SOLD

Using Positive Self-Talk
to Change Your Life

YOU ARE WHAT YOU THINK

Dr. David Stoop

In *You Are What You Think*, Dr. David Stoop shows you how to use self-talk to make positive changes in your attitudes and beliefs in order to

- choose healthy, positive thoughts
- respond rather than react to circumstances
- overcome guilt, anger, anxiety, and stress
- release the power of faith
- and more

Revell
a division of Baker Publishing Group
www.RevellBooks.com

Available wherever books and ebooks are sold.

Do you want change that lasts?
The first step is to change your mind.

In this practical and encouraging book, Dr. David Stoop shows you the true path to lasting change: the renewing of your mind.